# Elements of Game Design

# Elements of Game Design

Robert Zubek

The MIT Press
Cambridge, Massachusetts
London, England

© 2020 Massachusetts Institute of Technology

All rights reserved. No part of this book may be reproduced in any form by any electronic or mechanical means (including photocopying, recording, or information storage and retrieval) without permission in writing from the publisher.

This book was set in Stone Serif and Stone Sans by Westchester Publishing Services. Printed and bound in the United States of America.

Library of Congress Cataloging-in-Publication Data is available.

ISBN: 978-0-262-04391-5

10  9  8  7  6  5  4  3  2  1

To Matt
for everything

# Contents

# Acknowledgments

The idea for this book came from teaching game development courses at Northwestern University, and the first round of thanks goes to my students for whom this material was put together (initially as a set of course notes before it turned into a book) and who were the initial beta testers of this text. Special thanks go to Ian Horswill and to Northwestern University for supporting this class, and to Ethan Robison for his insights as a TA of the course.

My thanks also go to colleagues who kindly agreed to look over this text while it was still in very raw shape, especially Noah Wardrip-Fruin for extensive feedback and playtesting this text in his game design class, and to Chris Solarski and Randy O'Connor for detailed critiques. Additional thanks go to Ebyan Alvarez-Buylla, Peter Franklin, Tadhg Kelly, and Rob Lockhart for their thoughts and feedback, and to Gediminas Einikis for the character illustrations.

More thanks go to the various colleagues who discussed and questioned game design with me and with whom I learned what I know about games, at work and in grad school, through the various games we made together and separately. You are too numerous to list, but you know who you are. Thank you.

And the final round of thanks goes to my partner, Matt, for supporting my brash decision to write this book and supporting my nights and weekends at work once it became clear just how big of a hole I had dug for myself. But as the Leonard Bernstein quip goes, "To achieve great things, two things are needed: a plan, and not quite enough time." As game developers, maybe we can take some comfort in this, as we are perpetually short on the latter.

# Introduction

This text covers the basics of the process of game design. It is intended for newcomers to game design, especially students in introductory level classes.

The aim is practical. I want to introduce the reader to a process of creating new games and analyzing existing ones. Along the way, we examine a model for thinking about games on three different levels (from bare mechanics through dynamic behavior and gameplay to end-user experience) and how we can use these levels to simplify the design problem by dividing it into stages.

In writing this text, I wanted to describe the tools and techniques used by game designers working in the industry. As a game designer and developer, I felt that it was important to share with students the basics of the knowledge that we have collectively accumulated. Our industry is new, only several decades young, and it keeps evolving rapidly—but some of the foundations are starting to take shape. So now might be a good time to survey what we have learned so far in anticipation of building on it in the future.

## Game Design and the Scope of This Text

Games are syntheses of the work of many disciplines, and all parts must work well together to produce a great experience for the player. Interesting and engaging gameplay, visuals and visual design, music and audio design, user experience design for smooth interaction, technical design and implementation, and so on.

*Game design* is typically used in the industry to refer only to the design of the gameplay aspect. A design for a game is a kind of formulation for how the game should *work:* how it will behave, what the player will do, who the characters are, how they act when the player interacts with them, and so on. This is complementary to the visual design of how the game will look, or the technical design of how exactly all the pieces will be implemented, but it is treated as a separate practice. Gameplay design works with the other elements and brings them together.

There are many ways to approach the broad topic of game design, and this text focuses on a few specific motifs, as follows.

1. *Focus on models and vocabulary used in industry practice.* We will use the techniques and vocabulary used by practicing designers working on shipping commercial products. The game design community has developed numerous abstractions and mental models for working in this domain, as well as its own terminology, and this text seeks to introduce these as they are used in practice. There has also been a wealth of theoretical work in game studies and research, which introduces a variety of additional models and vocabularies; however, we will leave that work mostly untouched except for elements already adopted in industry practice.

2. *Focus on games as dynamic systems of gameplay.* We will be looking at the design of gameplay and gameplay-related elements. As previously mentioned, there is much more to contemporary games than gameplay: stories, characters, visual art design, audio design, and so on. But instead of discussing all of them, we concentrate on the *sine qua non* of games—the dynamic nature of what happens when players get a hold of the game and start interacting with it, and how to design this kind of dynamic gameplay to produce desired experiences. As for the other elements of game development, there are other, much better resources on art, story, or technical design in games.

3. *Focus on the design process, but not on the profession of design.* Similar to the above, we will focus on the work of designing gameplay, but we will not largely address the realities of the job of being a game designer. Working on a production team in a commercial environment brings with it many additional challenges: team communication, creative leadership, processes for generating and filtering ideas, evaluating commercial feasibility of design ideas, and so on. These challenges do influence game design, but we will largely ignore them here, since doing justice to commercial production issues would make the discussion far too complex for our purposes.

4. *Focus on game design, but not on game product design.* Game design is the process of figuring out what the game will be in terms of gameplay, but

product design is figuring out how to turn it into a successful commercial product—how it fits into the marketplace, how to market it and present it to an audience, how to sell it and what kind of sales or monetization model to use, and generally, how to make it successful in a very crowded market. Game design and product design are interdependent, and experienced game designers often develop a sharp eye for how product requirements inform game design, and how game design innovation can illuminate new product possibilities. However, product design is too advanced of a topic for this introductory text.

## Classroom Use

This text is intended to be an introduction to elementary game design concepts. It arose out of a compilation of class notes from my game development class at Northwestern University. However, the goal for the text is to be applicable in various contexts, from more theoretical design courses, to applied game development lab courses, as well as self-study.

The text begins by introducing the core model—that of player and designers experiencing the game design differently, and the three levels for thinking about games—and the subsequent chapters elucidate the individual parts of this model. The chapter sequence itself is very flexible, however. The current sequence recapitulates the ordering I used in my own introductory game development class:

- Chapter 1 introduces the model.
- Chapter 2 discusses player experience, and identifying design goals.
- Chapters 3 and 4 discuss ways to analyze lower-level mechanical details.
- Chapters 5 and 6 discuss ways to analyze higher-level gameplay, structure, and resulting player experience.
- Chapter 7 focuses on applying these elements when building a playable game prototype.

However, other types of classes might choose to order the elements differently. For example, a course that focuses more on theory of design might adopt a sequence that looks more like the following:

- Chapter 1 introduces the model.
- Chapters 5 and 6 discuss ways to analyze higher-level gameplay, structure, and resulting player experience.

- Chapters 3 and 4 discuss ways to analyze the lower-level mechanical details.
- Skip chapters 2 and 7.

The chapters should be amenable to different orderings as well, according to the needs of each course. In addition, this book is succinct so that additional materials can be pulled in as needed for instructors who wish to combine it with external readings on game design.

## Note on Exercises

Each chapter comes with a set of exercises intended for individual use and some design challenges that are best done in groups. Individual exercises are typically prompts for analysis or discussion, for example, asking the reader to analyze some game they know in the context of what they just learned in the previous chapter or chapters. These questions tend to be open ended, with the hope that they will be applicable to a variety of teaching contexts, including homework or in-class discussion, and students from a variety of backgrounds.

The text does not include exercises where students practice building entire games or game prototypes, since those exercises can be highly specific to the teaching context (different exercises would be needed for courses that focus on digital games as opposed to physical games, for courses that assume programming knowledge as opposed to no programming knowledge, and so on). For readers interested in physical design exercises, I wholeheartedly recommend Brathwaite and Schreiber (2009).

## Note on Style

In this text, I tend to use first-person singular "I" as myself, the writer, speaking on my own behalf, and use first-person plural "we" in the context of myself and the reader, working together through a problem or examining game examples. Phrases such as, "We now see that ... ," are used as rhetorical flourishes to highlight the trajectory that we, the writer and the reader, are taking while exploring the topic.

However, I would like to emphasize that the "we" is decidedly *not* intended to suggest that I am speaking for other game designers or developers. I would not dare to speak for them, and besides, it would be impossible as the game design community is highly heterodox and ever-evolving. Please consider views and opinions in this text as entirely my own.

## Note on Definitions

It has been customary for game design texts to start by defining the word "game," but I will resist this temptation.

Many definitions have been suggested over the years. Some popular ones include defining games as "conflicts in which the players directly interact in such a way as to foil each other's goals" (Crawford 2003, 8) or "a system in which players engage in an artificial conflict, defined by rules, that results in a quantifiable outcome" (Salen and Zimmerman 2004). Many more have been offered as well, and Sellers (2017, 90–96) and Salen and Zimmerman (2004, 73–81) provide many examples and excellent summaries.

These kinds of succinct definitions tend to be inaccurate, however, because they routinely fail to match the vastly heterogeneous variety of *things* that people call games. The word "game" is used to describe an enormous category of activities and artifacts, including arcade games (shoot-'em-ups such as *Arkanoid* or *Gauntlet*), action games (*Super Mario Bros.*, *Grand Theft Auto*), cerebral or puzzle games (*go, sudoku*), story-driven games (*The Curse of Monkey Island, Gone Home*), sandbox simulations (*SimCity, Minecraft, Dwarf Fortress*), realistic simulations (*Microsoft Flight Simulator, Forza Motorsport*), video game sports (*Madden, NBA Live*), real-world sports (*football, baseball*), card games (*poker, gin rummy*), collectible card games (*Hearthstone, Magic the Gathering*), parlor games (*Fictionary, Exquisite Corpse*), games of pure chance (*roulette*, various slot machines), strategy board games (*chess, Diplomacy, Risk*), strategy computer games (*Civilization, Master of Orion*), kids' board games (*Snakes and Ladders, Candy Land*), playground games (variants of hide-and-seek, or cops and robbers), augmented reality games (*Majestic, Pokémon Go*), freeform role-playing (LARPs), rule-based role-playing (*Dungeons & Dragons, Ultima*), open-world games (*The Witcher, The Elder Scrolls V: Skyrim*), interactive fiction (Inform- and parser-based games), hypertext stories (Twine games, *Choose Your Own Adventure* series), and various others that I skipped because the list so far already makes the point.

The problem with simple definitions is that they routinely fail to capture this variety and, paradoxically, end up excluding many famous games from being considered "games." For example, the definitions offered by Crawford or Salen and Zimmerman both reject some of the best-selling games of all time, such as the *SimCity* series, *Minecraft*, or *The Sims* series, as being "not games," based on nothing more than a declaration by fiat. This contradicts the actual, real-world usage of the word "game," and as such, they are inaccurate and inappropriate for use.

Second, and more problematically, inaccurate definitions can be taken as normative and used to deny new types of games their ontological status as games. There are numerous historical examples of this phenomenon. In the late 1990s, we saw arguments about whether simulation games like *SimCity* or *The Sims* are games or merely "toys" because they lacked clear goals and victory conditions. Similarly, in the early 2000s, casual games were debated as marginal games because they were very easy and lacked a meaningful physical or strategic challenge. In the late 2000s, this repeated itself with social games like *FarmVille* and mobile games like *Candy Crush*, accused of not being games because they were reductively simple yet addictive and allowed players to pay to skip any undesirable challenge. Then in the 2010s, the so-called "walking simulators" like *Gone Home* and hypertext games like *Depression Quest* became targets of debate about whether they are games, as their designers rejected traditional mechanics and systems in favor of storytelling and emotional experience. This phenomenon of using incomplete definitions of "game" to marginalize non-core games and deny the importance of their contributions seems to repeat itself with an unfortunate consistency.

A comprehensive definition seems elusive. Therefore, instead of a prescriptive definition, in this text we take a descriptivist approach: that games are what people who play games, who talk about games, who make games, and who enjoy games say they are. They may have some traits in common. They usually lack real-life consequences. They can incorporate pretend-play. They might make use of competition, goals, or observable outcomes, and so on—but these traits are not all necessary. The gamelike traits may be present but do not all have to be, and if the thing under consideration is *similar enough* to other things we call games, we will happily call it a game. In this manner, we follow Wittgenstein's approach to language (1959, paragraphs 66–71) and treat "game" as a description of a family of phenomena that resemble each other. They cannot be positively defined with a set of necessary and sufficient conditions, but we can identify when something shares many characteristics with other things we know as games and include it in the family.

With this preamble out of the way, we can now finally switch over to the main question that will drive this text: So, how to make those things?

# 1 Elements

> For a moment in time we leave ourselves; and when we return, sometimes expanded and strengthened, we are changed both intellectually and emotionally. And sometimes ... we experience what life has not allowed us. It is an incalculable gift.
>
> —Maryanne Wolf, "What Does Immersing Yourself in a Book Do to Your Brain?"

We all recognize the familiar, deep pleasure of being immersed in a book, a movie, a work of art. We seek out the way they enthrall us, confront us, make us experience the world through another's eyes. Different art forms accomplish it in their own ways, but they all have this mysterious power.

Games have this power too, as players know well. A familiar transformation happens when we allow ourselves to get immersed in a game: for a moment we leave ourselves and become someone else, and we experience their life, their world, their story.

Games also have an additional power. In games we also gain the ability to *act*. We can take on a different role in life. We become an adventurer, an explorer, a general—not through empathy, but *actively*. We embody that role, experience what it is like to act as them, to function in their world. We witness firsthand how our actions bring about consequences and learn from experience how that world works. This is a unique power of games, that they allow us to not just observe the world, but inhabit it, act in it— and perhaps change it.

This is also our task as game designers and the subject of this book: how do we create these experiences, these worlds for the player to inhabit and interact with?

## Design Process

When creating a new game, we may already have some basic ideas, what kind of a game it is, what the player will do, or how it will look. But we need to turn these ideas into the actual concrete details of the new game, building a new design from the ground up. Just like writers prepare for a book by writing plot outlines or sketching out characters, so do game designers use a variety of techniques for making a game: we plan out their mechanics and feedback loops, we analyze player actions at various frequencies, we match player motivations against the resulting experience, and so on—and, most importantly, we prototype and experiment.

This is what we will cover in this text: the variety of tools and processes used by game designers. No game springs into existence fully formed, games require a creative spark but also considerable technique and execution. In this book we focus on the latter and specifically the kinds of techniques used by practicing designers in the industry, like mental models, process descriptions, and ways of thinking that people found to be particularly useful in the process of creating new games.

## Games as Machines

We could look at games from a variety of perspectives: the storytelling or screenwriting perspective, or from art and visual design, or from cultural analysis, and so on. But because our focus is on creating gameplay and interaction, we are going to take a different approach.

We will focus on games as systems that the player engages with, games as *machines for playing with*. Here "machine" is a shorthand for a dynamic model, an artificial system of rules and interactions that players operate, not a literal physical construction. But what we want to emphasize is the reactive, dynamic nature of the game: the machine guided by its own rules, the player pushing on the machine as they act and explore their options, and the pull that the machine exerts on the player and forces them to react. It is this repeating push and pull within the boundaries of the game's rules that the player identifies as gameplay.

To see how these machines work, we will take them apart, and we will inevitably start noticing patterns. There are commonalities that show up across a variety of games, shared structural elements and shared solutions to design problems that we can identify. Each individual game might arrange them in a novel way, but the building blocks are common, and although new blocks appear over time, many are old and well known. Assembled together, this structure enables players to interact in specific ways and experience a particular kind of gameplay.

This is not the only way to analyze and understand games, but it is a useful one, and practicing game designers have already identified and named a variety of common structures and building blocks that show up repeatedly in design practice.

## Game Design Is User-Centered

When game designers talk about the craft, there is an unspoken assumption that the games we make are *for players to play*. This sounds like an obvious truism, but not everybody treats games this way. Mathematicians, for example, may consider games as problems to be solved optimally, ignoring the player.

But we take this as a central guiding principle: that games are meant to be played. And if games are created for players, we must take players and their experience into account from the beginning. The player must be at the front and center of our design process.

*User-centered design* is fundamental to game design. A game is designed as an experience, an interaction that gives the player agency and autonomy. Our design process approaches this by looking at three elements: the designer's goals for the experience; the game artifact that will bring it about; and, most importantly, the player who will be having this experience. They all need to work together in a conversation between the designer and the player via the designed gameplay.

So, where do we start?

That is what this text is all about. First, we start with an example.

## Motivating Example: *Poker*

We can use a popular game such as *poker* as a case study and take it apart to see what kind of pieces it is made of. Imagine sitting down with a group of friends and playing a few hands. What are the parts that make up this experience?

First, the basic structure. We have a bunch of game pieces that the players work with: cards, chips, a play table, and the various things that make up the physical aspects of the game. We can consider them as the *objects* or *nouns* of the game. Cards and chips are concrete objects, but there are also more abstract elements: one's hand of cards, one's turn to play, and so on. Objects also do not have to be physical. Online *poker* is made up of the same pieces as table *poker*, only virtual. We also have rules for what we can do with those pieces and at what times. Rules define what *actions* or *verbs* we can apply to those nouns—when to shuffle cards or how to deal them, what it means to ante up to get my hand, how I can place a bet or call someone else's bet, and so on. The game starts out in some initial *game state*, and then player's actions move the game from one state to the next. In the case of *poker*, we also have some rules that specify what it means for a player to win the hand, so that players can try to reach their winning states with the hand they have been dealt.

Once players sit down to play the game, they put those pieces in motion. The dealer starts by shuffling the deck and everyone chips in the starting ante so that the cards can be dealt. Players then take their turns, examining their choices, maybe placing bets on who has the better hand, maybe changing the cards in the hand, maybe calling or raising someone else's bet, and so on. At some point the hands are compared and one of them is determined to be the winner. And then they start all over again. This is the *gameplay*, the decisions, interactions, and activities that players are doing in the game. Gameplay does not have to be limited to just the game pieces, either. Players are calculating odds and reading other players' behaviors. They are bluffing and trying to get their opponents to fold. Maybe they are posturing or pretending. Other players are a huge part of gameplay in many games, and *poker* is especially known for mixing the elements of strategic thinking and planning, with the psychological challenge of figuring out one's opponents.

On top of that, we can talk about what players are doing and *experiencing* when playing the game. They are competing, for sure. But sometimes they also collaborate, such as by making and breaking temporary alliances. They risk their money and enjoy the thrill of gambling it on an unknown future. They strategize their next moves and enjoy figuring out what the best course of action is. And yet, at the same time, they chat and joke around, jockey for status, and have a good time in each other's company. This is the *player experience* of playing *poker*. Having fun, socializing, gambling, coming up with strategies, faking each other out—the combination is very strong and many players enjoy the interlocking aspects of this experience.

## Model Description

We will be using those three levels as a basis for analyzing games. We can summarize them briefly as follows:

- Players interact with different game *objects* and perform various *actions*
- Interacting with the game and other players over time creates *gameplay*
- Gameplay gives rise to specific *experiences* and *feelings* in each player

In the case of *poker*, the elements are cards, chips, and so on, and players can also talk to each other, which is another valid kind of game action. Based on the rules, players sit down and start dealing cards, betting, calling each other's bets, bluffing to confuse their opponents, and otherwise interacting with each other and with the evolving game state. This in turn lets players have fun by being competitive with each other, socializing but also fighting for the chips on the table, strategizing how to win over their opponents, or trash talking and posturing and generally enjoying the company of their friends.

Figure 1.1 shows the interplay between the basic objects and actions, the gameplay they produce, and the player experience that arises from them.

We can give these three levels names which are more general, as illustrated in figure 1.2:

- *Mechanics* are the game objects and actions that the player interacts with. They can be assembled into *systems* with specific properties.
- *Gameplay* is the process of players interacting with game mechanics.
- *Player experience* is the player's subjective experience of gameplay.

This is our basic model of interaction: players interact with mechanics and systems, which give rise to gameplay, which is experienced subjectively by players. In the following sections we describe in greater detail how we

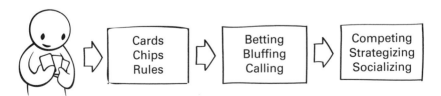

**Figure 1.1**
*Poker* example

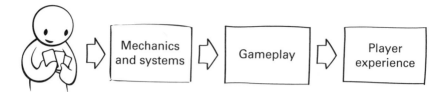

**Figure 1.2**
The basic model: mechanics and systems, gameplay, player experience

can use this model to understand both players' and designers' role in shaping this interaction.

This three-part division has grown out of the MDA model (Hunicke, LeBlanc and Zubek 2004) in which it is rooted. MDA calls the three layers *mechanics*, *dynamics*, and *aesthetics*, although the correspondence is not exact. The "Further Reading" section at the end of the chapter explains the similarities and differences.

### Designer's Role

Now let's put ourselves in the shoes of a game designer who wants to create a new game. The designer will typically have some experience in mind for the player, perhaps to have them enjoy being challenged strategically, or to have them enjoy a new story, or maybe to have them experience the fantasy of being a different person in a different time, and so on. The possibilities are many, but how can we bring this experience about?

Our challenge is that we cannot create this experience directly. We can only manipulate the basic, concrete pieces: the game rules, pieces, characters, and so on, which make up the game. We need to create a *game artifact* which, when played over time, will hopefully bring out intended experience.

This is a hard, second-order problem, as we are twice removed from the end goal. We are not simply crafting a static object; we are creating a dynamic machine which will behave in some way, and this behavior is what we hope players will enjoy.

### Designer's Process

If we look at how other things get designed, not just games but also software or physical objects, we often see two directions in the design process:

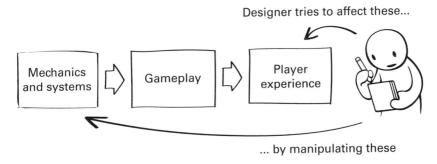

**Figure 1.3**
Designer's role: setting up mechanics and systems to produce desirable experience

- *Top-down design*, where we start with the main vision and goals, then divide it up into smaller pieces that describe how those parts work in greater detail, then divide those into even simpler pieces, and so on.
- *Bottom-up design*, in which we start by making the smallest possible thing that is a starting point towards our main vision. We then test and make sure that it satisfies our goals, and then incrementally build on top of that.

In game design, these two approaches look as follows:

- Top-down design starts with a desirable player experience and figures out how to split it up into various pieces. We figure out what kind of gameplay can generate this experience and then how to generate this gameplay from the variety of mechanics that we are familiar with.
- Bottom-up design explores the space, builds mechanics and systems first, and tries them out with real players, continually testing what kinds of gameplay and experiences are being produced.

In practice, neither of these works well in separation. Pure top-down design is difficult, because we are trying to design dynamic systems, and it is hard to predict how these will actually work when we put them in front of players. Similarly, with the purely bottom-up approach, it is highly experimental, but unless these experiments are guided by some vision of the player experience they may never converge into a coherent design.

The solution is to take a hybrid and iterative approach, working from both ends, creating a lot of top-down plans as well as bottom-up experiments, and, most importantly, building prototypes early and often to test these design ideas and try to get them to converge. This hybrid, iterative

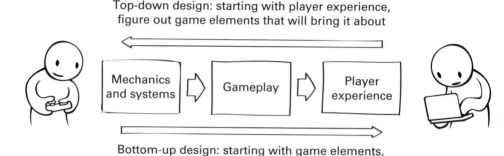

Top-down design: starting with player experience,
figure out game elements that will bring it about

Mechanics and systems → Gameplay → Player experience

Bottom-up design: starting with game elements,
figure out how to produce desired experience

**Figure 1.4**
Design approaches: top-down and bottom-up

process is something that game design shares with other areas of design practice (Brooks 2010).

### Player's Experience

The player comes from a different perspective than the designer. They do not know what experience we intended for them, instead they start with the concrete elements of the game—the mechanics, the game pieces, and the rules. They pick up the game and start playing.

The resulting experience of playing the game can vary wildly. Maybe they will experience a delightful, strategic challenge, or have a good time exploring the virtual world, or perhaps have a negative experience and get frustrated or bored. But all of these experiences come from *playing the game*, from having the variety of game pieces and rules and interacting with them (and possibly other players) as the player desires.

As is probably obvious by now, the player experiences not what the designer intended, but what the designer *implemented*. All that the player knows is what it feels like to play the game in front of them, with the pieces, rules, enemies, or challenges they were given. Designer's intentions are immaterial, save for how they turned out in the implementation.

There is also a tension between the designer's intentions and the player's agency. On one hand, the player plays in a world created by the designer and interacts with the mechanics and systems provided by the designer and purposefully set up in a specific way. But on the other hand, they have their own agency and ideas about what they want to do, which might not

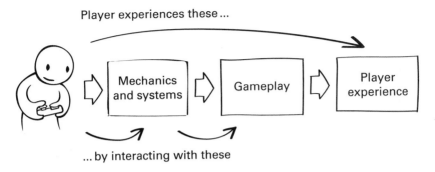

**Figure 1.5**
Player's experience comes from interacting with the game

be what the designer intended. What the player does in this world is up to them and, within the rules set up by the game, they have full freedom to take the game in whatever direction they want.

And so, gameplay ends up being an interplay between the player and the designer. Both the designer and the player contribute. The designer sets up an experience, and the player participates in it in a way that they want, collaborating with it or subverting it as they please. Sometimes the negotiation is successful and the designer succeeds in creating a desired experience. At other times, players find their own fun by undermining the designer's construction and turning it into something else they want instead. And sometimes the designer's careful structure simply fails and the whole experience falls apart. This interplay is a conversation, and it requires a degree of cooperation from both sides, as well as acknowledgement that there is no single "correct" way to play a game.

**Elements of Games Outside This Model**
So far, we introduced elements such as mechanics, systems, gameplay, and player experience. These are at the core of the discipline of game design, and we will discuss them in much greater detail in the following chapters.

But as any game player knows, there is much more to enjoying playing a game than just these elements! These are crucial for sure, but there are a number of other elements that will also strongly affect how the player will experience the game.

- *Visual design* of the game has a huge impact on the player's experience. This runs the gamut from world design, such as how the game world presents itself to the player or the characters and environments and everyday objects, to small scale design, such as the choice of fonts or how detailed the 3D models are.

- The quality of the *user interface* and its overall presentation will directly impact players as well. In computer games this includes user experience design, although in physical games it would include the tactile feel of game pieces or the richness of the game board.

- Tied closely to visual design is the choice of *setting* or context of the game—where the game takes place, what the player's role is, and so on. How the player feels about their pretend role in the game world will naturally color their feelings about the whole game.

- In story-based games, the developing *story* is typically very important. Scriptwriting elements such as characters and their motivations, the situations they find themselves in, and the plot being experienced by the player, as well as the more basic aspects like the quality of dialogue writing, will also affect the player's experience.

- In-game *music* and *sound design* have a huge role in video games, as do artistic decisions about music or the soundtrack. In some genres, music and sound design are absolutely central to the experience.

- *Technical design* elements are usually invisible to the player but will have an enormous impact in the quality of the player's experience, such as the quality of the AI that will challenge the player, or the types of multi-player matches that the platform makes possible.

… And so on.

We can try to map the variety of game elements that contribute to the player's overall experience, as shown in figure 1.6.

In this text, we only concentrate on designing mechanics, gameplay, and how changes in gameplay design affect the player, "all other things being equal." In other words, here we concentrate on *aspects of player experience rooted in gameplay*. But the player's *overall* experience is multifaceted, and gameplay is not the only factor (and in some cases, not even the major factor) affecting the experience with any given game.

## The Practice of Game Design

So far, we have used the term "designer" loosely to describe people who create elements of the game, the mechanics and systems that result in gameplay

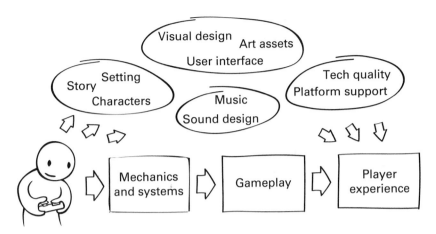

**Figure 1.6**
Examples of elements outside of gameplay that influence player experience

and player experience. Now let's introduce how the term "designer" gets used more precisely in industry practice.

## Game Design, Systems Design, Content Design

The term *game designer* in practice tends to describe jobs where the primary responsibility is designing rules for how things in the game behave and then usually implementing those rules.

This makes the job deliberately different from jobs such as art production (which focuses on visual design instead) or engineering (which focuses on code architecture and implementation). Although everybody on the team contributes to the player's experience, designers are specifically tasked with the responsibility for gameplay, which is to say, for how the game behaves and how the player interacts with it.

The designer's job further subdivides into categories:

*Systems designers* concentrate on overall mechanics and systems, for example:

   *Game rules*—what the nouns and verbs of the game are

   *Combat design*—how fighting works, with what units and weapons

   *Economy design*—the rules for how items and currencies change hands

   … and others

*Content designers* concentrate on the particular and individual game objects and actions, for example:

*Level design*—the particular environments where the game takes place

*Character design*—who the characters are and what they do

*World design*—the player's trajectory through the game and why it is interesting

... and others

The distinction between systems and content design can be fuzzy, especially since the same people usually do both kinds of design work. In general, *game design* is figuring how things ought to behave, the rules of interaction, and within this role, *systems design* is a subtype that concentrates more on figuring out the overarching and generic rules, and *content design* concentrates more on creating specific places, characters, or items, and rules specific to those contexts. Both types of design also need to be considered in the task of game tuning or making sure that the general rules and the individual elements are correctly balanced, as we will examine in chapter 4, "Systems."

On a related topic, UI design or visual design roles are not considered *game designers* in the industry. They are often considered *artists* because their task is mainly visual and not interactive (although UI/UX design is more interactive and cross-disciplinary). Similarly, designing the world may very well fall on the shoulders of *writers* who mainly write the overarching plot of the game, character backstories and motivations, and so on, but do not design rules for how the game world behaves.

Naturally, a single person can take on several roles at the same time, and, on smaller teams, the lead designer will routinely shoulder a variety of responsibilities. Also, some of the roles interact heavily with other disciplines. Content designers often work with visual design and storytelling, and systems designers often interact with engineering.

In this text, we will concentrate mainly on systems design. Content design is a very broad discipline in which a lot of knowledge is specific to styles and genres. For more information about content design, please see the "Further Reading" section at the end of the chapter.

**Discipline Interactions**

Design is one of the main pillars of game development, the other two being art (visual design and production) and programming (including software design and implementation). Game teams will also include efforts from other disciplines, such as writers or sound designers, as well as less game-specific disciplines such as business development or marketing.

The division into art, design, and programming is very commonly reflected in studio organization. Project organizational charts are often vertically divided among those disciplines. It makes sense for game designers to be grouped together under a design director because they are best equipped to evaluate each other's work and give feedback.

At the same time, these roles rely heavily on working with the other disciplines. We often find that actual game teams, in addition to the vertical divisions, are also simultaneously divided up horizontally into small cross-disciplinary "cells" or "pods." These are small units that combine contributors from all three disciplines to implement specific features from start to finish. In this text, we concentrate mainly on the design elements, but it is crucial for a game designer to also hone their skills on working with other disciplines, from art and content to programming, marketing, business planning, and beyond.

## Summary

In this chapter, we introduced the basic model which will be the foundation for the following chapters. The key takeaways are:

- In this and the following chapters, we will be looking at games as "machines," as systems of rules and interactions that players operate and which in turn react to players' actions. We will focus on how these machines work and how they can be analyzed.
- In this text, we will be looking at games on three levels:
  - *Mechanics*, which are the individual pieces that make up the game
  - *Gameplay*, which is the dynamic process of players interacting with the game and each other
  - *Player experience*, the subjective experience that comes from participating in gameplay
- Mechanics are the most directly accessible element. Players play the game by interacting with the mechanics, which gives rise to gameplay and the particular experience for the players. Game designers may want to evoke specific experiences, but they cannot create that directly. Instead, they have to craft mechanics that will result in specific gameplay and

experience when players interact with them. However, both mechanics and players can behave in unexpected ways. Design must account for this as best it can.

- In the practice of game design, we can distinguish between *systems design* of broad rules, mechanics, and systems, as *content design* of particular, individual elements that the players will encounter. Here we concentrate on the former.

- Finally, this text concentrates on the design of gameplay, but we must also keep in mind that other elements of game production also have an enormous impact on the player and their enjoyment and experience. Here we will only discuss player experience in terms of how it arises out of gameplay.

Based on this three-level model of game design, the book's chapters are going to look into these levels in the following order.

- In chapter 2, we start from the top level, and examine different kinds of player experience, and the various ways in which we can analyze what brings it about.

- Next, in chapters 3 and 4 we switch over to the bottom level and look in detail at mechanics, what they are, how they work, and how they combine to form systems.

- Then, in chapters 5 and 6 we will look at the middle layer—how those mechanics and systems lead to gameplay, how this gameplay can be analyzed, and how it leads to player experience. These chapters present a kind of synthesis between the experience that the designer desires for the player and the mechanics that will actually bring it about.

- Finally, in chapter 7, we zoom out to view the entire process, how designers use these analytical tools in game production and the prototyping process that turns the initial kernel of an idea into a working design.

## Further Reading

### Formal Tools

Game designers have been sharing their experiences since the early days of commercial board and computer games—describing techniques, postmortems, or lessons on what worked and what did not. However, with the growth of the industry in the 1990s, there has been a growing desire for game designers to share more than just learnings from individual products but to discover and document general design knowledge in game design. Perhaps the best-known call to action for such general design research is the "Formal Abstract Design Tools" paper by Doug Church (1999), followed by a response "I Have No Words and I Must Design" by Greg Costikyan (2002). Both are available online and worth reading through in entirety.

## MDA

Many general models have been developed over the years to show how games can be decomposed and analyzed. One of the popular ones is the MDA framework (Hunicke, LeBlanc and Zubek 2004), which is the precursor for this work. The author of this text is one of the authors of the MDA paper.

Readers familiar with MDA may have noticed that it similarly divides up game design work into three aspects. In MDA, these are the eponymous *mechanics*, *dynamics*, and *aesthetics*. This text shares the three-part division as well as an emphasis on the higher-order design problem, where players and designers only interact with the game artifact itself via its mechanics.

This text does not present MDA as is for several reasons. Most importantly, there are stark terminology differences between MDA and contemporary design practice. Using the term *dynamics* to describe gameplay is virtually unheard of in practice, which would impair communication for readers attempting to interact with designers on the job. Similarly, the term *aesthetics* in MDA is used to mean "the aesthetic experience of interacting with game systems," but in the game development industry, it is used almost exclusively to talk about visual aesthetics and not about the player's experience of gameplay. Keeping the MDA vocabulary would be confusing.

Second, the dynamics part of MDA is too ambiguous, as it includes both the analysis of dynamic systems composed of mechanics as well as the analysis of how players interact with the game. Although they share a common root (they both describe behavior), contemporary design practice finds it useful to speak of game systems as its own class of phenomena, different from but related to gameplay loops and the player's experience of the interaction.

Finally, MDA's model of the designer and the player being on the opposite ends of the MDA chain is idealized but confusing, as the actual iterative design process approaches a game from both ends simultaneously. I hope that this improved model helps address some of these shortcomings.

### The Practice of Design

On the topic of design in general, not specific to games, *The Design of Everyday Things* by Norman (1988) is a highly recommended introduction to product design and how psychology informs design choices. *The Design of Design* by Brooks (2010) is also an approachable introduction to general design theory.

For more information about game design, especially content design and the everyday work of designers in the industry, including many interviews with designers in the industry, two recent books stand out: *Game Design Workshop* (Fullerton 2008) and *Challenges for Game Designers* (Brathwaite and Schreiber 2009).

Beyond gameplay design, game designers should be acquainted with the basics of visual design, as it commonly has very strong impact on the player's performance of the game and the experience of going through it. For a great introduction to visual design in games and how it impacts gameplay, *Interactive Stories and Video Game Art* (Solarski 2017a) is full of practical tips and advice.

This text also focuses on the practice of designing games as artifacts and does not focus on the external concerns of game industry, games as a medium, games as narratives, or the intersection with larger cultural and social practices. For those concerns, additional books worth reading are *Rules of Play* (Salen and Zimmerman 2004), especially parts three and four, as well as the essay collections *First Person* (Wardrip-Fruin and Harrigan 2004), *Second Person* (Harrigan and Wardrip-Fruin 2007), and *Third Person* (Harrigan and Wardrip-Fruin 2009).

### Individual Exercises

#### 1.1. Nouns and Verbs

Pick a multiplayer game you know well and perform a similar analysis to the *poker* example. Pick a card or board game so that it is not too complex, maybe on the level of *poker*. Now describe the following:

a. What are the verbs and nouns of this game? What do players do, and what do they do it with?

b. What is the gameplay? What happens when players come together and play? What kinds of activities do they engage in?

c. What is the player's experience of playing? Is it enjoyable, and how does gameplay contribute to this?

### 1.2. Elements outside the Model

Take the game you described above in 1.1. Now consider elements other than mechanics and gameplay that affect the experience of playing the game. Prepare a list. What are they? For each one, describe in one sentence how you think it contributes to your enjoyment of the game.

## 2 Player Experience

We all have our favorite games. Each one of us remembers games that cap-
tured our attention: games that fascinated and enthralled us, games that we
binged on in short, intense episodes, or games that cast a spell that made
us return to them time after time. This is our job as game designers: to
create these kinds of experiences for the player. We want our players to be
enthralled and intrigued, or perhaps challenged and inspired, or enjoy the
gameplay and their experience in other ways.

But why would players want to play our game? What is it about the
game that will be so enthralling? This question is key to the game designer's
role. It is also surprisingly difficult to answer.

In the previous chapter, we introduced the general model for analyzing
game design and discussed how designers can try to produce a desirable
experience for the player. This is where we start our analysis. In this chapter
we examine player experience, we discuss different ways of thinking about
players, and we analyze what kinds of motivations players have when playing games.

### Experience Is Relative

What do we find enthralling about the games we play? I can try to answer
this question for myself first: why do I like what I like? If I think of my
favorite games, I can easily rattle off a variety of reasons. For example, I
love *Civilization* games, but why? Maybe it is because of the strategy challenge, because I can grow a mighty empire but also have to defend it against
enemies from the outside and economic collapse from the inside. Or the
*SimCity* series, in which I enjoy the process of building a huge sprawling
city that gets more and more difficult to keep running as it gets bigger and
forces me to destroy what I have created in order to create more.

Everyone can also come up with their own favorite games and a multitude of reasons why they enjoy them. At the same time, if I asked others whether they like *Civilization* or *SimCity*, they might tell me that they do not. Or if they do, they might have different reasons. Maybe somebody enjoys the combat and warfare aspect of *Civilization* rather than empire-building and management, the opposite of my reasons for liking the game.

To paraphrase the old adage, enjoyment is in the mind of the player.

And although the maxim is quotidian, it feels very intuitive. We would expect every player to have their own likes and dislikes. This also leads to a few implications that will serve as a starting point:

1. *Players play games because they enjoy them*. This is a bit of an obvious truism. They clearly find something interesting about the game that captures their attention and fits their mindset. They feel motivated to play it. If they were not motivated, it would be a chore rather than a game. But in what way are they motivated? We could say that players are "having fun" or that a game is "fun," but that word is dangerous to take in its general sense. The everyday word "fun" implies that ebullient, cheerful feeling of joy, but a game does not have to be joyful in that sense to be enjoyable. Players often look forward to a difficult challenge and persist in the face of frustration, hardship, and exhaustion. They may also engage with a game about a painful subject such as death or disaster. So, we cannot assume "fun" as the reason, and instead we will talk about people *enjoying* a game as a shorthand for feeling motivated to play, whatever their reasons are.

2. *Different players find different kinds of games enjoyable*. For example, some people definitely enjoy strategy games. The games tickle their mind in some way, and they are motivated to spend their time on them. But clearly not everybody likes strategy games, and some may dislike them, perhaps intensely. This is the same with action games, racing games, and so on, each of us has our own idea of games that we like or dislike. In short, there is no game or genre or style that everybody will enjoy. Likewise, we are unlikely to meet a person who enjoys all games, genres, or styles.

3. *Different players may enjoy the same game for different reasons*. I may enjoy historical aspects and economic management in *Civilization*, but another player might prefer the combat and warfare aspects. There is nothing inherently more "correct" about what I enjoy about a game compared to how someone else enjoys it. However, that does not mean that the game supports all of these equally. If I start up *Civilization* expecting a

deep story and character development, I will be disappointed, as the game is definitely oriented towards strategy and management. And although some large-scale games try to support many different aspects of gameplay so that different kinds of players will still find something that speaks to them, they are unlikely to be equally strong at all of them.

4. *Whether or not a game is enjoyable is relative.* Following directly from the previous points, if everyone's experience is different, it makes no sense to ask whether a game is "enjoyable" by itself, objectively. The same game can be enjoyed or not enjoyed by different players or for different reasons, so we can only ask whether it's *enjoyable for some specific players.* Later on, we will try to generalize this and ask whether a game can perhaps be enjoyable for some specific *types* of players. This generalization will be very useful, but the reference to the audience must always be there.

These points will not surprise those with prior exposure to arts, as contemporary art practice realizes there is no such thing as aesthetics without reference to the participants, where they are coming from, and how they interact with the piece. But for our purposes, we will leave the philosophy of aesthetics untouched beyond pointing out that it is relevant here.

These intuitions have direct consequences on game design. We cannot make a game that will be objectively "enjoyable" or "fun." We cannot even hope to make one that's objectively "better" than another without assumptions about the audience or some evaluation criteria. We also cannot expect to make a game that everyone will like or that nobody will dislike. Also, those who like it (or dislike it) will have varied reasons and motivations for how they feel. What we *can* make is a game that is enjoyable in specific ways for particular players. We can and should talk about how specific players will experience our game and how we can guide them to have the kinds of experiences we want them to have.

Consequently, we need to consider who our audience is, and why they might enjoy our game from the very first moment in the design process.

## What Do You Enjoy?

We know that enjoying a game is highly subjective and dependent on the player as well as the game. Now we can go one step further. Once I have identified a game that I find enjoyable, I can start asking myself what *specifically* do I find enjoyable about it?

If I look at *Civilization V*, for example, which is an intricate strategy game, I can start to rattle off a wide variety of personal reasons:

- I like the progression of starting out with a small empire and growing it into a superpower.

- I enjoy building out big cities and managing them, making sure everybody is happy.

- I dislike combat, but I enjoy having powerful armies and using them in negotiations.

- I like the rush of having to react to unexpected situation and strategizing future moves.

- I really like science research and developing new technologies and more powerful units.

- I enjoy the visual style and that it looks a bit like a board game.

- I like the historical context and playing against actual countries that existed.

- I find it fun to play as a real historical figure like Napoleon or Alexander the Great.

… And so on.

**Figure 2.1**
Screenshot from *Civilization V*

This is my personal motivation list—it describes what I find enjoyable and why I like the game. Any of us can come up with similarly varied lists if we consider any of our favorite games, and we could also create similarly detailed reasons for not liking some games.

But a huge laundry list is not very useful. We would benefit from trying to express it in more general ways so that we can see if it applies to other games or other players.

## Building a Naive Taxonomy

To start with, I can make a simple *categorization* of those points above. Forming groups or taxonomies can help bring out underlying structure.

I will group my reasons for playing *Civilization* into categories, and then try to figure out if something about those categories is particularly interesting. A naive grouping might look something like this:

- *Gameplay elements:* what I do in the game, what kinds of game nouns and verbs I have to work with, the systems built from them, and the challenges they present—especially those around strategy and economic management. If I reskinned the game to have a different presentation but kept the gameplay elements, they would still be enjoyable in the same way.
- *Fantasy elements:* the historical settings, the game characters, levels, units, weapons, and other elements. Our civilization and its history are very interesting separately from the game rules and mechanics.
- *Presentation elements:* visual design, art style, how people and places look, how they're animated, the style of the place and time in history.
- *Story elements:* characters and their stories, what they do, their personalities and motivations can be intriguing like the way stories in movies and books pull us into their made-up worlds.

Assuming this naive taxonomy, I can then try to describe how well *Civilization* matches it:

- I quite enjoy *gameplay* elements in this game, and there is a rich variety of them.
- I enjoy the *fantasy* of being a historical ruler, and the game supports it very well.

- I'm ambivalent on *presentation elements*, although the game has very good presentation.
- I like games with a *narrative*, but the game does not have many.

And just like that, we created our first theory of *player motivation*. We analyzed some player motivations, and we tried to group them into a more general theory. From this taxonomy we can try to make predictions and try to test them. For example, if I find other games that have strong gameplay and fantasy elements, I could try to predict that I might also like them based on this theory.

However, let's make no mistake—this naive taxonomy is *terrible*. It suffers from numerous defects, the worst of which is that it is based on just my own intuition from my own experience with just one game and does not take other games or players' experience into account. Can I make any predictions about how others will enjoy *Civilization* based on this theory? Not really. So, this is not going to be useful in figuring out how to make games for other players.

But this is a good starting point for looking at other, better theories of player experience.

## Player Theories

We have seen that individual experience is not enough. My own motivation profile explains me, but it does not explain others. We would prefer a motivation theory that would help us understand whether and how other people might enjoy some particular games, and maybe even tell us why they enjoy them.

There have been numerous attempts to find such models, to divide players up into various player types in order to better understand the connections between them and to understand what motivates them. We will talk about three different approaches: designer theories, authored user personas, and empirical studies. In this section we discuss the first two and then turn to empirical studies in the next section.

### Designer Theories

As we observe players playing games, it becomes immediately obvious that different players derive different kinds of enjoyment from playing a game or prefer some kinds of games over others. Game designers routinely evaluate their games with many different players and testers in a variety of contexts, and some designers have been sharing their observations about patterns in player behavior.

In this chapter, we will call these *designer theories* of player behavior—that is, theories created by designers based on their observations and intuitions about the different types of player motivations. Below we cover two theories which are perhaps the best known: the model of player types by Bartle and the model of individual player motivation by Koster.

## The Bartle Model

Probably the best-known game designer taxonomy is the model by Bartle (1996). Based on his experience running multiplayer online text games ("MUDs"), Bartle observed that players of online games tended to fall into particular routines when interacting with each other. From those routines, he postulated that players in MUDs fall into four broad categories based on motivation:

- *Achievers*, motivated mainly by increasing their levels and achieving goals
- *Explorers*, motivated by exploring the game world and learning how it works
- *Socializers*, motivated by storytelling, talking with other players, roleplaying
- *Killers*, motivated by competition, victory, domination, and also trolling

The Bartle model suggests that these different kinds of players derive their enjoyment of the game unequally from different sources. If I were an "achiever" kind of a player, I might enjoy parts of the game that focus

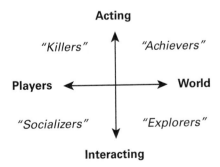

**Figure 2.2**
Bartle's (1996) diagram of the four character types

more on goals and rankings, and a "socializer" might not care about those so much and instead draw enjoyment from the company of other players.

This also implies that the groups behave very differently from one another, which could potentially get them into conflict. For example, achievers might get annoyed when teamed up with socializers, because the latter do not "play to win." So, in the context of multiplayer games, it becomes very important to make game worlds that provide something for each of them and to keep them balanced.

Even though initially created only to describe players in MUDs, Bartle's taxonomy remains popular, as it gives readers a handy, immediately usable guide for figuring out what motivates different kinds of players and how to make the game better for them. However, as those categories are based on intuition and informal observation, a game designer needs to replace them with observations from *their own player base* interacting in their own particular game, as those populations may have motivations that are different from the above four.

### The Koster Model

Raph Koster's book, *A Theory of Fun* (2004), postulates a model of player motivation that derives from a single fundamental drive: the joy of learning and getting better. As long as we are encountering new challenges, overcoming them, and learning successfully as we go, we are going to be engaged with the game and enjoying it. But in order for this to work, the challenge has to be both intrinsically interesting to us (fortunately, humans are curious creatures and we find many things interesting), and "just right" in terms of difficulty (neither too easy nor too hard).

The fun of learning is related to the psychological *theory of flow* and personal motivation, which extends across many areas of human endeavor not just games (Csikszentmihalyi, Abuhamdeh, and Nakamura 2005). The theory proposes that all people can experience a state of enjoyable deep engagement, the eponymous "flow state," when faced with a challenge that is interesting and at the right level of difficulty. Since this kind of enjoyment is tied to player interests, player skill, and game challenge, it neatly explains why the same game might be very differently experienced by different players. For example, a complex strategy game such as *Civilization* will be more enjoyable for experienced strategy players rather than players who are inexperienced with the genre and its conventions, even if both groups are equally interested in it, and similarly for other games that require quick reflexes, or planning and strategic thinking and so on. (We will cover flow theory in more detail later, in chapter 5, "Gameplay.")

This understanding of "fun" is also linked to notions of action spaces and state spaces, which we will touch on in chapter 3, "Mechanics." The "fun" is connected to how well the player has learned how their actions affect the game's state space. The game is not fun if it is either too predictable or too unpredictable—and it is most fun when the player is actively learning how to affect the game state through their actions.

More designer taxonomies do exist, and we will touch on them again in the "Further Reading" section at the end of this chapter.

## User Personas

Although designer theories try to understand player motivations in the abstract, a different approach might be to understand players contextually as individual people living their lives and use that to try to infer their possible motivations.

This approach is used in the creation of user personas. These are a popular tool in the design and marketing of all types of products and are typically written out as short vignettes of different kinds of users who would be using the product. Those vignettes may come either from conducting surveys of users of existing products and seeing what commonalities emerge—or by just *imagining* who the most relevant users would be based on experience.

In a user persona, we try to capture who our users are, in detail, as people living their daily lives, and imagine why and how they would want to play the game. For example, if we were working on a game like *The Sims*, we might imagine a number of different types of players, maybe collapsed into three or four stereotyped personas. We could write them out as follows:

- Alice is a teenager who plays the game for a few hours after school. She enjoys building the house and the stories of the different families living in the neighborhood and is also an avid fan of the different themed expansion packs.
- Bob is a young professional in his mid-twenties. He plays strategy and management games on a regular basis and switches between them regularly. When playing, he tends to be competitive and finds new ways to surpass his previous scores and achievements.

- Carol is a professional and a mother of two grade school–aged children. Even though she likes games, she can only play them occasionally, for maybe an hour at a time. She enjoys the interior decoration aspect of the game, often redecorates her houses, and creates new in-game items.

These user stories may seem clunky and awfully stereotyped, and they often are. (For example, why is the male a competitive one, but the interior decorator is female and a mother of two? Is this a reflection of actual player types or a reflection of the writer's particular view of the world?)

But that is deliberate. The point is to put together these sketches of imagined stereotypes, faulty but interesting, in order to imagine their motivations and behavior. The user persona is an *intuition pump*, a story that helps the designer get an insight into the imagined player and answer questions like "Who are we making the product for?" and "Why would they want to buy it?" It helps us use our common-sense intuitions to understand our players.

This makes them very useful in helping designers focus the scope of the game. For example, if we conclude from this exercise that our players will typically be working adults who play our game after work, we may want to make it easier to play it in shorter sessions, make multiplayer optional, reconsider any online competitions that require participation on workdays, and so on.

User personas are also different in that they make no claims about being general theories. Personas are written from scratch for each specific product and for each specific audience, and they are not intended to make a point beyond that.

### Empirical Models

Designer theories, like those mentioned above, are primarily driven by the authors' intuition and experience with a large number of players. They are distillations of their own firsthand observations. But we could approach these questions from a different angle, removing the designer from the loop. In particular, we could ask players to self-report about how they feel about various situations and activities (in games or otherwise) and see whether some of these answers are correlated and cluster together into groups.

We will describe two interesting and relevant empirical studies that have direct impact on game development: first, the popular *Big Five model* for describing personality types (independently of games); second, some recent empirical studies of player types specifically in computer games; and finally, we will describe how the two tie together.

## The Big Five Personality Model

We all know that we are different from each other, that we have our own specific personalities that influence how we might act in different situations—this much is common sense. But as designers, we may wonder, is there a way to categorize these personality differences and perhaps understand or even predict how different types of people might behave in a given context?

There have been many personality models proposed throughout history, from ancient theories of the four bodily humors to more recent folk theories such as the Myers–Briggs model, but they share a similar defect: they try to fit people into preconceived taxonomies. In contrast, modern psychology prefers personality models where categories are derived empirically, rather than assuming some specific categories a priori.

The Big Five personality model is probably the most well known and well tested of these data-driven approaches. It is based on the analysis of how people describe themselves and others, and on the words people use to describe common reactions and emotional states. The Big Five model identifies five principal personality factors or dimensions as follows (John and Srivastava 1999, 121):

- *Extraversion*—energy in social settings, sociability, but also assertiveness
- *Agreeableness*—prosocial orientation, altruism, trust, modesty
- *Conscientiousness*—goal-directed behavior, impulse control, following norms, organizing
- *Neuroticism*—negative emotionality, feeling anxious, nervous, tense
- *Openness*—desire for breadth of experience, originality, complexity

Each of these dimensions also has a flip side—for example, the other side of extraversion is introversion and the lack of sociability and energy in social setting. Every person's traits can be described as falling somewhere on the positive or negative side of each dimension. Personality traits also appear to be quite stable during adulthood, in spite of changing life circumstances.

Traits seem to have some association with behaviors and life outcomes, although this association is not strong and very much depends on context. For example, in employee testing, conscientiousness was found to generally correlate with job performance, but in more specific job contexts other traits can predict more specific outcomes, such as extraversion correlating with success in sales and management positions. Effects of traits in other contexts have also been studied, such as in school performance or healthy living (John and Srivastava 1999).

However, Big Five is not commonly used in game design. Although it can be inspirational when thinking about what might motivate different kinds of players, this model by itself is too broad and difficult to apply to the very specific task of game design. On the other hand, in the following section we describe some new findings that connect personality types directly to gameplay preferences and open up a promising direction for further study.

### Yee's Gamer Motivation Profiles

Beyond personality studies, there is recent work that tries to answer the question of game playing motivations much more directly.

Nick Yee at Quantum Foundry has been organizing a long-running survey of game players, asking them to rate their preferences for various aspects of gameplay. Questions in the study were based on twelve types of in-game motivations, sourced from a variety of models, including psychological studies of motivation as well as more traditional designer theories (Yee 2016, 12).

### Action Aspects

*Destruction*—the enjoyment of chaos, mayhem, guns, explosives

*Excitement*—the enjoyment of intense, fast-paced games

### Social Aspects

*Competition*—the enjoyment of competition with other players

*Community*—the enjoyment of interacting and collaborating with other players

### Mastery Aspects

*Challenge*—the enjoyment of overcoming challenges, preference for games of skill

*Strategy*—the enjoyment of games that require careful decision making and planning

### Achievement Aspects

*Completion*—the desire to complete every mission, get every collectible and hidden item

*Power*—the enjoyment of becoming powerful in the context of the game world

### Immersion Aspects

*Fantasy*—the desire to become someone else, somewhere else

*Story*—the importance of an elaborate storyline and interesting characters

### Creativity Aspects

*Design*—the appeal of expression and deep customization

*Discovery*—the desire to explore, tinker, and experiment with the game world

After asking players to self-rate along those twelve types of motivations, Yee found consistent correlations in players' reports of how much they liked the different aspects of games. Players who expressed higher preference for one of these motivations would also express higher preference for one or two related ones: for example, people who reported enjoying strategy were much more likely to also prefer challenge, but they were less predictable along other dimensions such as community or fantasy.

The study also presents multiple charts showing those correlations collapsed into 2-D graphs, in which correlation strength is translated into

| Action | Social | Mastery | Achievement | Immersion | Creativity |
| "Boom!" | "Let's Play Together" | "Let Me Think" | "I Want More" | "Once Upon a Time" | "What If?" |
|---|---|---|---|---|---|
| **Destruction** Guns. Explosives. Chaos. Mayhem. | **Competition** Duels. Matches. High on Ranking. | **Challenge** Practice. High Difficulty. Challenges. | **Completion** Get All Collectibles. Complete All Missions. | **Fantasy** Being someone else, somewhere else. | **Design** Expression. Customization. |
| **Excitement** Fast-Paced. Action. Surprises. Thrills. | **Community** Being on Team. Chatting. Interacting. | **Strategy** Thinking Ahead. Making Decisions. | **Power** Powerful Character. Powerful Equipment. | **Story** Elaborate plots. Interesting characters. | **Discovery** Explore. Tinker. Experiment. |

**Figure 2.3**
Diagram of player motivation types (Yee 2016, 12). Reprinted with permission. Copyright 2016 Quantic Foundry

proximity between the points. Figure 2.4 shows just one of them, the chart for Western European players. However, interestingly, the correlations seemed to be roughly consistent across players from different countries and cultures (Yee 2016, 14–16).

Based on these correlations, authors proposed grouping them into three *clusters of motivations* that are often present together.

1. *Action–social cluster:* Excitement, destruction, community, competition. This covers the energetic, intense, gregarious play, and gaming with other people.
2. *Mastery–achievement cluster:* Completion, strategy, challenge. This covers different ways of progressing through the game, attaining mastery, and power.
3. *Immersion–creativity cluster:* Story, design, fantasy. This covers different ways of relating to the story and design of the world.

The clusters show that there may be regularities in what motivates players. For example, the proximity of strategy and challenge (or story and design) suggests that more players enjoy the two together, compared to the

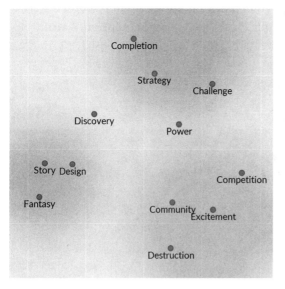

## The 3 Clusters

1. Action-Social
2. Mastery-Achievement
3. Immersion-Creativity

## Bridges

- Discovery is a bridge between Immersion-Creativity and Mastery-Achievement.
- Power is a bridge between Action-Social and Mastery-Achievement.

**Figure 2.4**
Diagram of proximities between player motivations (Yee 2016, 14). Reprinted with permission. Copyright 2016 Quantic Foundry

number of players who enjoy challenge and design. Additionally, the discovery and power motivations sit in-between, as "bridges" with a broader player appeal.

The clusters also highlight some surprising proximities. For example, why would players' enjoyment of competition and community would fall in the same group, since they seem opposite to each other? However, authors suggest this makes sense if we consider them both as reflections of a person's extraversion personality trait, whether competitive or collaborative.

Although the data suggests consistency across languages and countries, at this point we do not know the causes for these proximities and clustering, whether it is based on exposure to existing games (styles, genres, etc.), or whether it reflects player personality on a deeper level. But though the model is early in development, the overall approach is valuable—starting by collecting data about what players enjoy and then trying to extract groupings from this empirically observed data. These groupings can help us, as designers, have more certainty about what kinds of experiences our players might find enjoyable.

## Player Motivations and the Big Five

In a follow-up study, Yee asked people to fill out both a player motivation survey and a personality survey, and then sought correlations between gamer motivations and their personality profiles.

The resulting correlations were not strong, but some interesting patterns emerged (Yee 2016). They show potential correlations between three of the five personality types and some gamer motivation types, and the other two personality types did not match up:

- Higher openness correlated somewhat with higher preference for fantasy, story, design, and discovery.
- Higher extraversion correlated somewhat with higher preference for excitement, competition, and community.
- Higher consciousness correlated weakly with higher preference for strategy.
- Agreeableness and neuroticism did not seem to correlate strongly to gamer motivation types, but the reasons are unclear.

As mentioned above, these correlations between personality and gamer motivations help illuminate some of the unexpected clustering results. For example, competition and community are very different motivations, yet they both relate to extraversion and the desire to interact with other people (whether by trying to cooperate or dominate).

Interestingly, these results go against the popular perception that games are escapist fantasies where we pretend to be someone we are not. Yee argues the data suggests the opposite, that the games we play reflect our personalities and what really appeals to us.

In other words, that *games let us more fully express ourselves as we already are.*

## Experience Design

So, what is it that makes a game enjoyable?

We have covered a number of different ways of looking at this problem, and we have seen that "being enjoyable" is not a pure property of the game. Rather, enjoyment is a function of both the game and the particular player who is playing the game.

We can try to develop some ideas of why different things appeal to different people and analyze what particular players like by applying a number of player experience models. Designer theories are usually easy to apply and function as great sources of ideas. Similarly, writing out user personas can help us as an intuition pump to understand the player better and imagine their experience from a first-person perspective. We can also use existing empirical studies to see how players can be classified using their self-reported preferences, to understand what players enjoy and how their motivations cluster together and support (or not support) each other.

These conceptual models can help us anticipate player experience. Even though we cannot create experience directly, this knowledge of player types and motivations can help predict how they might react to the kinds of gameplay and mechanics that we will create for them.

### Questions to Guide Experience Design

Suppose that we have a game in mind that we want to make and we want to start analyzing player experience. We need to move from the general question of "what makes a game enjoyable" to "what will make *my game* enjoyable," and then on to "what will make *my game* enjoyable to *my players*."

In short, when we design a new game, we need to interrogate our game idea in the context of players.

- *Who am I making the game for?* Is it a specific type (or types) of players, or is it a game that should have mass appeal to many, various types of people? How do I know who the players are? We can look at it either through the lens of player motivations or by assembling player personas to try to imagine who our stereotyped players are. But this is probably the first question that needs to be answered, as it will influence the others.

- *What will they enjoy about playing this game?* This ties directly to our audience. Given our assumptions about who I make the game for, what is it about the game that they will enjoy? What aspects of the game speak to this audience or to other audiences? Game designers are often voracious players of various types of games and tend to answer this question from experience. We can also use something like the player motivations model to figure out what kinds of motivations will be satisfied by this game. This will give us some idea about whether the game matches what we expect from our players. Answering this question is easier for games that are made for a specific player type, such as niche games or genre games. For mass market games, we still need to know why players will enjoy it, but we may have to divide players up into multiple subgroups based on the different things they will find appealing. This is when user personas become particularly useful.

- *What else would they enjoy that's not in the game? What would they not enjoy?* For example, if our game is a war game focused on competition and strategy, it might be beneficial to enhance community aspects by adding guilds or chat rooms. But if we considered adding a story element instead, we should consider whether this would enhance the enjoyment for our target players. In other words, given what we know about the audience for this game, can we extend the game in interesting ways to satisfy a related player need? And conversely, what might be some unrelated player motivations that we should be careful about so that our game does not end up unfocused, trying to be too many things to too many people.

These questions are just starting points for exploration, but they will force us to address the main questions, of who our audience is and how we think they will experience the game we make.

**Experience Archetypes and Genres**

In the discussion so far, we have already hinted many times at the existence of genres. We use terms like *war game*, *strategy game*, and *management game*, among others. These are popular labels, and they are legion: *real-time strategy*, *first-person shooter*, *arena shooter*, *role-playing game*, *open-world sandbox*, and so on. The precise definitions can be fuzzy, but both players and makers usually know what we mean by them.

Genres are shortcuts for describing what kinds of player experiences can be expected.

Very often, this means specifically mechanics, systems, and gameplay. For example, if I hear about a new *tycoon game*, just saying the name of the genre conjures up some expectations about what mechanics will be used and what I should expect out of playing the game—namely, lots of management and number crunching, economic simulation, strategic and competitive elements, probably a single-player game without a social component, and so on. Similarly, I can understand what it means to call something an *open-world RPG*, or perhaps a *squad-based tactical first-person shooter*, and so on.

Genres are also convenient in the process of *making* a game, because they help us quickly resolve a large number of design decisions, which otherwise might need to be tested out and prototyped. The choice of genre will help constrain the choices of gameplay and systems to a smaller, more manageable subset. For example, if we are making an open-world sandbox game, we know a lot about who the player is in the game, what they will do, what nouns and verbs we might need to implement, and so on. We do not need to answer these basic questions. Since the foundations are settled, we can move on to building an interesting and novel variation on top of them.

On the other hand, cross-genre or genre-bending games can also be very interesting because they merge different families of solutions into a novel shape that defies expectation. They are also tricky, since cross-genre designs bundle together different sets of design solutions, and it can be hard to take apart mechanics from different genres and then put them together in a way that works together well. But when it works, it has the potential of creating something quite novel and reaching different groups of players who have very different motivations.

## Summary

In this chapter we introduced techniques for analyzing player experience to understand what motivates players and what they might find enjoyable. The key takeaways are:

- Experience is relative. What is enjoyable for some players is not going to be interesting to others, and different players may enjoy the same games for different reasons. Consequently, we should not expect to make games that are "objectively" enjoyable or fun. That kind of experience is always relative to the *particular players* and their motivations.

- To understand what makes games enjoyable, we should first examine players and what motivates them. We can try to build *player theories* to help us predict how specific player types will react to some specific experiences.

- Several *designer theories* exist that seek to characterize player motivations based on designers' own experience creating games and observing player behavior. Developers also use *user personas* to try to tease out stereotypical player behaviors and motivations from user studies.

- Recent studies by Yee produced an empirical model based on large-scale player surveys of player preferences along twelve different motivation types, leading to several preliminary conclusions:

  - The study observed some clustering of motivations into three broad categories (*action*, *mastery*, and *creativity*), each of which contain several motivations that support each other. However, each individual player's motivations inevitably vary and different players may exhibit different combinations of them.

  - A weak correlation might exist between a player's reported motivation cluster and their personality aspects as reported on the Big Five model, but this requires much more validation.

  - Knowledge of player motivations can help us understand how players who have those motivations will react to our intended gameplay design, and we can use it to try to anticipate player experience.

After this foray into player experience, we will switch over to mechanics and start discussing the gritty details of how all this can be implemented. Coming up next in chapter 3, "Mechanics," we take a look at the low-level details of how games work. And through the following chapters 4 through 6, we will examine how all this builds up to produce the kinds of player enjoyment and experience that we discussed here.

## Further Reading

On the topic of "enjoyment" and "fun," the jury is still out on what is the most precise terminology. Early on, designers used to abuse the word "fun" to describe player experience, with assumptions about how the player *should* feel. This was counteracted by a wave of critiques, the best-known ones by Doug Church (1999) and Greg Costikyan (2002), opposing the use of the word "fun" as too specific and too limiting. This text uses the term "enjoyment" as perhaps less loaded but still highlighting that the subject commands interest, attention, and voluntary engagement. After all, the things we enjoy feel to us like play, not work.

### Player Psychology

On the topic of personality studies and the Big Five personality model, John and Srivastava (1999) provide a very detailed examination of the history and current status of the Big Five model. For interested readers, a preprint version is also available online (John and Srivastava n.d.).

Beyond personality, other perspectives on player psychology are also fruitful. On the level of specific psychological effects, *Getting Gamers* (Madigan 2015) describes the many ways in which individual psychology, such as loss aversion or sunk cost fallacy, can greatly influence player behaviors, and how they are often used in game design. On a more macro level, *Virtual Economies* (Lehdonvirta and Castronova 2014) describes games as economic systems and how to use economic modeling to understand the incentives and motivations that explain why players behave how they do.

Theories from outside of games, such as the self-determination theory, also help shed light on the question of what motivates people in general, in their life, of which games are only one element. For self-determination in particular, Ryan and Deci (2000) describe this general framework— grounding human motivations in the desire for competence, autonomy, and relatedness. Ryan et al. (2006) propose applying it to predict game enjoyment, and Deen (2015) examines in detail how it can be applied to game design specifically.

## Designer Theories

Beyond empirical studies, there have been numerous designer theories proposed over the years. In addition to Bartle and Koster models described in the chapter, we can point out two that are particularly worth looking at. For additional taxonomies, please also see Yee's "Gamer Motivation Profile: Model and Findings" (2016).

The Caillois taxonomy (1962) is one of the earliest models of player motivation, and it divides the kind of player experiences into four main categories:

- *agôn* (roughly, competition)
- *alea* (roughly, excitement of chance)
- *mimicry* (what we now might recognize as fantasy)
- *ilinx* (roughly, the rush of high-speed physical activity)

The Caillois method was based on intuition and observation, combining the study of culture and anthropology. Numerous later taxonomies of "fun" can trace their roots to this intuition-based approach. Though not used in design practice, this taxonomy might be of historical interest.

In contrast, Lazarro's *Four Factors* model is a recent taxonomy of experiences, and, even though it is broader than just a player motivation model, it provides great insights into the different facets of gameplay experience. Four Factors splits up player enjoyment of the game into four quadrants:

- *hard fun* ("fiero"), which relates to challenges and overcoming them
- *easy fun*, which relates to curiosity and the joy of exploration
- *serious fun*, which relates to excitement and intense focus
- *people fun*, which relates to social bonding and taking care of people

The corresponding study provides practical details on how these experiences are related to various emotional responses and gives actionable advice on how those responses can be elicited from specific game design elements (Lazzaro 2004). It is recommended to readers interested in specific examples of games and emotions they bring out.

## Individual Exercises

### 2.1. Experience Is Relative

Pick one of your favorite games. Discuss the following: Why do you enjoy playing it? List out your top three gameplay aspects (mechanics, activities, systems, etc.)

that you enjoy in the game, and top three non-gameplay aspects (visuals, theme, story, characters, music, etc.), with a one-sentence description of each.

Imagine another player who enjoys the game as well but has different taste or different priorities—their favorite parts of the game are different from yours. Imagine and describe this player. Who are they, and what are their top three reasons in each category?

### 2.2. Bartle Model

Consider some multiplayer game that you have played (online or local multiplayer). Do you see Bartle types reflected in players in that game? Do you fit into one or several of the types? Or are you motivated by things that Bartle's model does not capture?

### 2.3. User Personas

Go back to your favorite game from 2.1. Imagine several different "types" of players who might enjoy this game in different ways and write out their user personas: who they are, what they enjoy, and how they fit the game into their lives. Think beyond your own experience and try to imagine a variety of players from different walks of life.

### 2.4. Yee Model

Consider your own game playing habits in the context of the twelve categories of player motivations proposed by Yee. Which of the twelve motivations reflect your own motivations the most? Which of them are you indifferent to? Do you see yourself in any of the three clusters, or are your motivations more varied?

### 2.5. Questions to Guide Experience Design

Consider one of the games you know well. Answer the three questions from this section about that game, putting yourself in the game designer's shoes:

a. *Who am I making the game for?* Specifically, mention what kinds of player motivations it satisfies and what kinds of motivations are not addressed by that game.

b. *What will they enjoy about this game?* Which elements of gameplay (which activities, mechanics, and so on) are central to satisfying those player motivations?

c. *What else would they enjoy?* If we were to extend the game in some way, what might be a good direction that would work well with our expected player motivations, and build on existing gameplay?

### 2.6. Experience Archetypes and Genres

Pick a genre you are familiar with. Which of the Yee's player motivations would you expect to be satisfied by games in this genre? Which motivations are less related to the genre?

Think of a game you know that tries to be cross-genre or merging genres. Does it satisfy the player motivations from both of these genres, or only satisfy some of them and fail to satisfy the rest?

# 3   Mechanics

In the previous chapter, we examined player experience, how players perceive and interact with games, and the kinds of motivations they might have when playing. Now we turn to the topic of creating these experiences for the player, starting from the basic level of mechanics.

As game designers, we seek to create experiences. Whether we want to challenge the player's strategic abilities, or perhaps have them experience a captivating story, or give them an adrenaline-packed action scene, or some other type of an experience, it is our job to translate this vision into an actual game that they can play.

Our challenge is that we cannot create this experience directly. We can only manipulate the basic, concrete components—the game pieces, rules, characters, and various other elements with which the player will interact— and plan it all out in a way that leads to a good experience for the player.

We now shift our focus to these basic elements. In this chapter we will talk about mechanics separately from other design aspects, and in the next chapter we will discuss how they compose and form systems for the player to interact with. In future chapters we will move on to discussing the resulting gameplay, but for now, we will focus on just the basic elements.

## Mechanics as Building Blocks

The term *mechanics* describes the basic activities in the game and the rules that govern them. Let's start with some examples. In a game like *poker*, mechanics would be activities like dealing cards, betting, and calling—these are the basic things that players do when playing the game, governed by the rules of the game. In a game like *Monopoly*, the basic activities include moving around the game board, buying and owning property, collecting rent

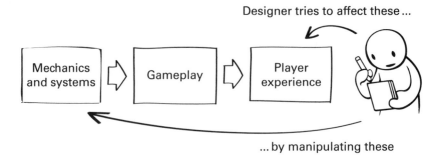

**Figure 3.1**
Designer's role: setting up mechanics and systems to produce desirable experience

from other players, and upgrading property with houses and hotels. Or in a fighting game like *Tekken*, the basic activities might be melee and ranged attacks, defending via blocking and parrying, timing effects like attack windup and cooldown, or advancing or retreating for strategic advantage.

And so, we will consider mechanics to be the basic activities and mechanisms that are afforded to the player. Mechanics bottom out in implementation—the paper or plastic pieces and rule books of board games, or the algorithms and data structures in computer games. However, those plastic pieces and rules are not mechanics themselves; they are components. These components must *come together in specific and meaningful ways* to make up mechanics. For example, in *poker*, an individual card is not a mechanic and neither is putting chips into the pot. But calling someone's hand is a mechanic, a basic activity in the game composed of those simpler elements like cards and chips.

## Composition of Mechanics

We mentioned that mechanics are made from simpler components, composed together in specific and meaningful ways, and we can now describe those constituent parts in more detail. The most typical component types are:

- The *pieces* that can be acted on or manipulated
- The kinds of *actions* that can be performed with pieces
- The *rules* that determine what actions can be done when, with what pieces, and what the outcomes will be

*Game pieces* are likely the most intuitive element. Physical games are full of concrete pieces to manipulate. *Poker* has chips and cards, the table, and the pot of money in the middle of it. *Chess* has the game board, board pieces, and sometimes a game clock. *Settlers of Catan* has the game board, improvement tiles, resource cards, and dice.

Games can also have *virtual pieces* that represent physical ones. The character sheet in a role-playing game is full of virtual swords and battle axes, gold pieces, potions and spell books, which are only symbols on paper (or screen), but they function as pieces that can be manipulated. Game pieces can also be *abstract*. A player's "hand" in *poker* is just a grouping of other pieces, but it is sometimes useful to treat it as a single "thing." Also, *poker* and *chess* and *Settlers of Catan* all have a notion of a "turn" that is in possession of one of the players, which is meaningful because most actions are only available to the player who has the turn, and yet there is no object, physical or virtual, that corresponds to it.

*Game actions* are the flip side. If we have game objects, we should be able to do something with them. *Poker* players draw cards, ante up, and bet money. *Chess* players move their pieces on the board, take the opponent's pieces or lose their own, and sometimes exchange pieces like with pawn promotion. *Settlers of Catan* players roll dice to randomly choose a tile to harvest, they collect resources, trade, and build improvements. There is an infinite number of actions that could be defined by the game designer. Actions can affect pieces, move them on the board, modify their attributes, exchange them, remove them, produce them, and so on, in a myriad of ways that are specific to each game.

*Game rules* then specify how exactly those actions are allowed to work. *Chess* rules for instance, specify how the specific pieces can move on the board, or how piece capture works, in standard circumstances as well as *en passant*, and so on. Some games have simple rules: both *chess* and *go* are well known for sparse rules that nevertheless give rise to great combinatorial complexity. Other games may opt for much more complicated rules, with war games and collectible card games like *Magic the Gathering* leading the pack in complexity.

Rules, actions, and pieces are all intertwined. When we talk about "drawing from the deck" in a card game, that describes an action and relevant game pieces, and it relies on some game rules which are often spelled out explicitly, but sometimes can be assumed from context. An explicit rule might be that only the player holding the turn can draw a card or that they only draw one card. But some rules are so common that they do not get spelled out—for instance, that the player must always draw from the top of the deck, not the middle, or that the card goes into the player's own hand and not someone else's hand.

These kinds of components are useful in a variety of ways, not just in constructing mechanics. For example, rules of *chess* include regulations about what it means to win or lose a single game of *chess*, and in the context of ranked matches, they also define how to compute one's ranking score. These victory conditions are not mechanics, at least not in our understanding of the word. They are the goals which game players try to achieve using mechanics, and they form a part of a *metagame* which we discuss later in chapter 6, "Macrostructure." In short, we can think of game rules as a large set of various regulations about the game. They include rules for how actions and pieces interact, but also any other additional regulations that are desired.

### The Language Metaphor

A common metaphor for game mechanics is to compare them to human languages.

- Game pieces are like *nouns*, since they describe things.
- Game actions are like *verbs*, since they describe what happens.
- Game rules are like *grammar*, since they describe how nouns and verbs can be put together.

The metaphor is widely used, and it is common to use a question like "what are the player's nouns and verbs?" as a quick shorthand for "what are the items the player can work with or manipulate, and what are the kinds of actions and activities they can engage in?"

This metaphor also gives us ideas that there may be additional, auxiliary components to consider when we design mechanics.

- *Adjectives* that modify nouns: a *weak* armor compared to a *strong* armor
- *Adverbs* that modify verbs: jumping *quickly* compared to jumping *slowly*
- *Prepositions* that modify relationships: sitting *at* the table compared to *under* the table

We will come back to the idea of "modifiers" in a later section when we discuss specific examples of resource management mechanics.

**Example: Exploring *Monopoly***

To illustrate decomposition into mechanics, we can look at the game *Monopoly* and see what kinds of mechanics we can identify. We have already discussed the basic elements.

1. *Pieces that a player can manipulate:* a game board, dice, pawns, cash, properties, houses, hotels, sets of random event cards, etc.

2. *Actions a player can perform:* rolling dice, moving on the game board, landing, buying, paying rent, drawing random cards, etc.

3. *Rules that govern the game:* which actions can be performed given what context; what resources are needed, spent, gained; and what happens as the result.

We can try to tease out the individual combinations of objects, actions, and rules by iteratively questioning the game about how it works.

**Who am I as a player?** I am represented by a game piece on the game board.

**What do I do?** I move on the board, and then react depending on where I land.

**How do I move?** I roll two six-sided dice and move clockwise that number of tiles.

**How do I react after landing?** It depends on the tile type. If I land on someone else's property, I pay rent based on property characteristics.

**How do I compute this?** There is a base rent and modifiers that change depending on whether it is part of a set and whether it has improvements.

**What is a set?** A collection of adjacent tiles of the same color, owned by the same person.

**What is an improvement?** A house or a hotel placed by the owner.

**How does this affect rent?** A chart determines how rent changes due to sets or improvements.

... And so on. There are many, many more details we could list out.

As we can see, this kind of a Socratic dialogue with a game artifact can get detailed. But we already identified some basic mechanics of *Monopoly*: the mechanics of movement on the board, the rent mechanic for collecting money when the player lands on someone's tile, the matching mechanic of collecting neighboring tiles into a matching set for extra rent, and so on. And when we make a new game, it is necessary to figure out all of the mechanics and decompose them into pieces, actions, and rules so that we can commit them to a rule book or encode them in computer instructions.

## Games as State Spaces

Related to game mechanics, we should also introduce another set of terms that game designers use, such as *game state*, *state space*, and *action space*. These are used to talk about how a game evolves over time and the player's perception of what they can do and how they can affect this trajectory.

### Game State

As the designer Sid Meier once quipped, a game is a "series of interesting decisions" (2012). The crucial element of game design is understanding player's choice and how it changes the game over time. A game of *poker* or *chess* is not static. As players perform actions with the game pieces, the situation and players' fortunes change.

To describe the trajectory of a game over time, designers often borrow terminology from cybernetics and automata theory. They speak of the game and its players as a dynamic system with *internal state*. As players interact with the game and with each other, their actions change the state of the system, which in turn causes players to have to adjust their decisions and take more actions, which further change the state, and so on.

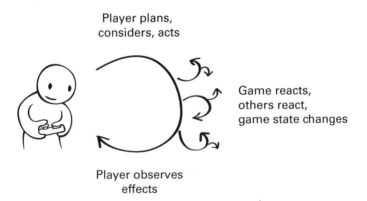

Player plans,
considers, acts

Game reacts,
others react,
game state changes

Player observes
effects

**Figure 3.2**
Player actions produce reactions from game systems and from other players, to which the player must react, forming a continuous loop.

In other words, we can say that

- *Game state* is the total state of all game pieces and their properties at a point in time.
- Actions in the game cause *transitions* between game states.

Game state may be fully or partially observable. *Chess* is an example of a game with *fully observable* state. If we look at the state of a chess board at some point in time, the game board fully describes the current state of the game. We can take a picture of how the board looks, then reconstruct it at another time or in another place and continue the game as if it had never been interrupted.

Most other games have hidden information, however, which means the current state is only *partially observable*. In a game like *Monopoly*, some information is available to everybody (such as which properties are owned by which player), some is only available to a single player (I could be concealing how much money I have), and some is hidden from all players (the order of random cards in the deck). All this information, visible and hidden, comes together to make up total game state. If we wanted to save the game state to reconstruct it later, this hidden information would need to be saved as well.

Hidden state is exceedingly common in computer games, since it is a powerful way to increase the strategic complexity of a game (such as in puzzles, strategy games, and other such), to create dramatic tension by hiding pertinent information (such as in combat and horror games), and sometimes even to mislead the player for narrative purposes.[1]

## State Spaces

From this perspective, a game is a series of game state transitions over time. In *chess*, the number of possible states and transitions is huge—the player often has many possible actions to choose from, and the game *could* transition into various possible states. But as the game progresses, each player can only pick one action per turn, and so they will navigate only a narrow trajectory through this space.

Looking at all the *possible* states the game *could* be in, we can add a few more definitions:

---

1. See Solarski's "The Unreliable Gamemaster" (2017b) for examples of hiding or revealing information to guide the narrative.

- The *state space* is the set of all states that the game could be in, connected by actions that transition from one state to the next.
- The *state space size* is the total number of states in the state space, or, in other words, the number of different states that could be reached from the initial game state.
- The *branching factor* for a state is the number of transitions (actions) out of that state.

Informally, we can talk about state spaces being *dense* or *bushy* when each state has a relatively high overall branching factor, or *sparse* when it is relatively low.[2] What counts as "dense" is relative to the genre and expectations. For example, children's board games are not expected to be nearly as dense as strategic board games for adults.

Space density and action set size both affect how players perceive the game. A sparse game that does not offer a lot of interesting decision points (say, *tic-tac-toe*) will not be as interesting as a denser game. This is, again, very audience-specific. Younger children love *tic-tac-toe* because its simplicity is a better match to their cognitive skills, which are still developing. Similarly, in the other extreme, a dense game might be more interesting, but *too dense* of a space will overwhelm a new player with choices they do not yet understand. The question of "how dense is too dense" is very subjective.

Even in sparse games, however, the total state space is routinely incomprehensively large. Size calculation for the simple game of *tic-tac-toe* seems straightforward: nine choices for player one, each of them followed by eight choices for player two, each followed by seven choices for player one, etc., for a total of 362,880 possible permutations (although that includes invalid or redundant states, so the actual useful subset of the space will be much smaller).

At least the state space of *tic-tac-toe* can be exhaustively enumerated and searched. The state space of *chess* or *go* has such a huge branching factor that it is impossible to search exhaustively even by the most powerful computers (and *chess* and *go* playing software must resort to shortcuts or heuristics to try to cut down the state space it needs to reason about).

---

2. Some designers (Elias, Garfield and Gutschera 2012) also speak of "game trees," which are game state spaces that contain no loops—in other words, when the game state can never repeat itself, such as in *tic-tac-toe*, or in many card games. These kinds of state spaces are traditionally called "trees" in decision theory as well as computer science. Admittedly, the term "bushy" makes much more sense when applied to trees than to spaces.

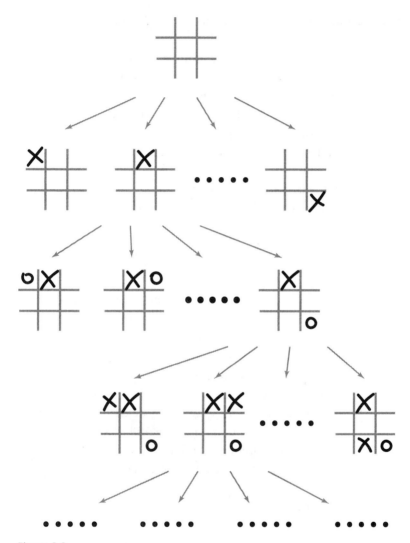

**Figure 3.3**
Illustration of a small part of the state space of *tic-tac-toe*

### Action Spaces

State space contributes to the combinatorial complexity of a game, but how these states are connected via actions, or the topology of the state space, influences the player's feeling of agency and what they can do in the game world.

*Action space* defined formally is the set of all actions that are available to the player. However, game designers also routinely use the term informally, using "player's action space" to mean the set of *actions available at the present state*.

For example, in *chess*, the overall action space would be the set of all possible moves ever, but informally, the current action space is just the set of moves available to the player right now. If players sit down for a new match, white gets the first move, but their immediate action space is tiny: sixteen different pawn moves and just four possible knight moves, out of a much larger set of all possible actions. It is not until later that the action space "opens up" more.

In this text, we will use the informal term *action space* to refer to the contextual set of actions available in a given state, and use the term *overall action space* to mean all actions.[3]

Action space size is very important, and directly influences the player's perception of game complexity. In a game like *tic-tac-toe*, the initial action space consists of nine possible moves, then reduces to eight, then seven, and so on—which is ever-decreasing and not very satisfying compared to a game like *chess* (or even *checkers*) where the action space is much more complex.

Secondly, as we already discussed, action space can vary over time, which is very interesting for the player. In *chess*, the action space in the beginning is very limited but it opens up mid-game as the player expands their control over the game board only to collapse back down in late-game stage.

Part of the enduring appeal of many games is the challenge of *controlling future action space*—in other words, planning well ahead to make sure we are ready for future opportunities and do not "box ourselves in" with a suboptimal situation because of poor choices we made early on.

### Perceived Action Spaces

Action space describes actions that the game makes available to the player. However, player's *perception* of what actions are available is just as important. Here are some examples of how this can differ from the player's actual possible actions:

---

3. Some designers use different labels to avoid this ambiguity, for example Upton (2015) uses the term *action horizon* to describe actions available immediately and in the near future, and others (Wright 2003) (Salen and Zimmerman 2004) use the term *possibility space* to describe the combination of actions and states contextually available to the player.

- *Unrecognized actions.* As a player, I might not realize some actions are available. As a new player in a fighting game like *Tekken,* maybe I have not yet learned how to perform blocking or dodging maneuvers, so I do not even know that I should consider them.

- *Excluded actions.* Even if I know about actions, I might reject them out of hand because they are clearly contrary to my goals or strategies, so they may as well not exist. I *could* shoot myself in the foot instead of shooting my enemy, but why would I even consider that?

- *Illusory actions.* I might also think some actions are possible. even when they are not. While walking on a dangerous ledge, I might fear that a false step will send me falling off of a cliff, when in reality the designer placed an invisible barrier there.

We can describe this as the player's *perceived action space,* that is, the set of actions they think they can or should perform at the given time.[4] What the player *thinks* they can do in any given situation greatly influences their experience in the game.

Real and perceived actions can be different and this is often exploited for dramatic effect (for example, suggesting that some situations are dangerous even when in reality they are not). But they must overlap at least somewhat, otherwise the game will be unplayable. If the player routinely fails to perceive what they can do, they will not be able to play the game, and if they consistently perceive actions that are not available, they will feel frustrated when they find out they were wrong.

## Explicit and Implicit Mechanics

Although it is possible to write out the rules for *Monopoly* or *chess,* it is vastly harder to write out the rules governing a computer game, whether a strategic game like *Civilization* or something more action-oriented like *StarCraft,* or especially an arcade game like *Tekken.*

This is the distinction between *explicitly* and *implicitly defined* mechanics. Explicitly defined mechanics are what we would encounter in a physical game, like *Monopoly* or *poker*—all actions and pieces are described in the rule book and the player can see everything that the game has to offer on the table in front of them. In these games, players play the game knowing all

---

4. Similar to the previous footnote, Upton (2015) uses the term *intent horizon* instead.

**Action differentiation.** In general, it is important that the player perceive a large action space. But beyond mere quantity, those actions should also be interestingly different from each other, and the more significant the differences, the better. For example, we could imagine casting different kinds of spells in a fantasy game.

- Spells that have different names but the same cost and benefit
- Spells that have similar but different costs and benefits
- Spells that have vastly different cost and benefits

The latter ones will be increasingly more interesting to the player. Choices in the first case are *illusory*. There may be multiple surface manifestations of the options, but they all lead to the same outcome, so they all represent the same transition in the state space. In the latter two cases, the choices are different, which will push the game in different directions—and the larger the differences and the more interesting the cost–benefit analysis, the more interesting the choices become.

For games that are meant to be replayed, it is crucial to keep the player's action space well differentiated with varying costs and consequences for the various actions. If a game is only meant to be played once, illusory or similar choices may be appropriate and interesting, but on multiple play-throughs players will quickly realize when those differences are only surface deep.

about how the game works, and even if they do not remember the details, everything is fully accessible and can be looked up.

Implicitly defined mechanics are much more common in video games. These rules are not known to the player ahead of time and often only exist in the computer code that implements them so they cannot be inspected. When the player starts out, they only know some mechanics (from the tutorial or watching other players), and as they play the game, they discover the rest and learn how they all tie together. For example, in a fighting game like *Tekken*, different characters have different types of moves the player can discover by practicing and learning from mistakes. Or in a war game, they may run into a new enemy with unit types that they have never seen before, and then they must figure out how those units work in order to counter them.

Implicit mechanics can offer a high level of surprise and discovery that is difficult to match in fully explicit games and the learning element can be very rewarding. In those kinds of games, the player is learning what kinds of mechanics become available over time and how to best use them to their advantage. However, this effect is sensitive to implementation details because hiding the game's rules can make it far more challenging than a game with explicit mechanics which are plainly visible to everyone.

Some games exist in between those two extremes. For example, collectible card games like *Magic the Gathering* have fully explicit rules for the game, but each card can also extend them. And since there are scores of rare cards and players need to buy those cards separately to access those rules, we can treat them as mostly implicit. Similar situation happens with "legacy-style" board games that come with secret rule packs that must be opened at a specific time and permanently change the game's rules, even for future sessions. Or for a very different example, a computer war game might be usually played as if its mechanics were implicit, having the player discover them as they play through the campaign, but an extensive manual might also exist for hardcore players who want to take the time to research the mechanics in depth.

The difference between explicit and implicit mechanics is also the reason why it can be difficult to use paper prototyping for computer games. We will discuss this in greater detail in chapter 7, "Prototyping," but in short, paper prototypes are small prototypes of parts of a game implemented using common physical media like paper cards and tokens. They are appealing because it is much easier and faster to create throwaway prototypes this way than through writing code to play on the computer. However, though this works for prototyping explicit mechanics, they are a poor fit for prototyping implicit mechanics, especially those based around physical activity or complex resource management.

## Examples of Families of Mechanics

Armed with some shared terminology, we can now discuss a number of examples of game mechanics across different kinds of games.

An unknown number of mechanics have been created (to say nothing about mechanics which are yet to be invented), so we cannot possibly try to enumerate all of them. As an industry, we even lack a shared, common taxonomy of the different types. The field of game design is too young to have settled on one, although some work has happened in this direction (see the "Further Reading" section at the end of the chapter).

Even so, we can talk about mechanics in terms of broad families. In this section we will discuss four families of mechanics in greater detail and then mention some more families that will be discussed only very briefly.

The following families of mechanics are very common and appear in a variety of games across time and genres, so we will discuss them in greater detail.

- *Control mechanics:* how the player is represented in a computer game and how the player's physical inputs are translated into controlling the game, their character, or other aspects
- *Progression mechanics:* giving the player feedback about their own performance in the game and changing the game in response to the player's progress
- *Uncertainty mechanics:* the role of uncertainty (not knowing what will happen next), the variety of the different sources of uncertainty such as randomness or hidden information and how that affects the gameplay
- *Resource management mechanics:* resource manipulation and ownership, such as mechanics around items, currencies, or resources that can be owned in the game and how things can be converted from one to another, or perhaps used up and consumed

There are, of course, many more types of mechanics—such as those specific to play formats, genres, or platforms. Here is a quick list of some examples:

- *First-person shooter mechanics,* specific to action combat games and deal with weapons and their properties, detailed input management (such as how aiming and navigation works), or the different types of team roles, goals, and dynamics
- *Racing mechanics,* such as in a car racing game, including mechanics of the physical simulation of the vehicle and how it responds to the player's actions, the race track and weather conditions, and so on
- *War game combat mechanics,* which describe how the different kinds of military game pieces act on each other, role of terrain or cover, and even more abstract military concepts such as the role of surprise in determining outcome
- *Real-time strategy mechanics,* which focus on managing squads in fast-paced top-down tactical combat, as well as building bases and managing supply and production chains

- *Multiplayer mechanics*, which concern balancing the game to be fair to all players, yet introducing different challenges, such as by introducing asymmetry which then quickly leads the discussion towards mathematical game theory

… and many more

These latter mechanics families overlap quite a bit with each other and it would be interesting to pursue them in depth. However, we will not discuss these latter kinds of mechanics here, since they are very numerous and context specific.

Instead, let us look at the four families of general-purpose mechanics mentioned at the beginning of this section: control, progression, uncertainty, and resource management.

## Control Mechanics

Many computer games are oriented around avatar action. In these games, the player controls an avatar that fights, runs, flies, shoots, and acts inside the game world. This is a shared element of games across many genres, from fighting games like *Tekken* or *Soul Calibur* to platformer games like *Super Mario Bros.* or *Prince of Persia*, from arcade games like *Pac-Man* or even *Asteroids* to story-focused games like *Uncharted* or *Journey*, and many others.

Action-oriented games in particular tend to reward quick reflexes and accurate, masterful performance. Consequently, if the game's handling of players' actions is clunky and inhibits their performance, that will be very perceptible to the player and it will feel wrong. Even if they cannot explain quite what is wrong with the game, players may complain that the controls feel "floaty" or "mushy" or "jittery," that the camera always gets in the way, or they may be getting frustrated and not even know why.

The following are the "three Cs" of action games (McEntee 2012):

1. *Character:* who or what the player's avatar is; what it can do in the game world; and whether the actions make sense, are fun to engage with, and are understandable

2. *Camera:* what the player can see and how well the camera follows the action, showing everything from the most useful angle and not getting in the way

3. *Control:* how well the player's controller input translates into character actions, whether it responds intuitively and accurately and is easy to pick up and learn

The rules and attributes that define these behaviors can be called *control mechanics* or *movement mechanics* or *combat mechanics*, depending on the particular game's focus.

The first two are probably the most intuitive. Some games have a *character avatar* that represents the player, and if the character cannot do interesting things or the player cannot learn or figure out how to play using this character, we can imagine the negative experience this would generate— frustration, boredom, or a feeling of not being in control, which works against masterful performance.

*Cameras* are another element, and they can be first-person (looking through the avatar's eyes) or third-person (looking at the game world from the outside). A first-person camera can only see ahead of the character, and the limited field of view can both frustrate and build tension. A third-person camera can see more, including what is behind the player, but issues around camera movement are tricky. Typically, we want to make the camera move by itself and follow the action in the game so that the player is not burdened by having to manage the camera while also playing the game. But making the camera "smart" when needed (making it look at the right thing at the right time yet also be controllable by the player), is quite difficult and a huge amount of work goes into making camera movement so good that it becomes unnoticeable.

*Control* is the third element—how the player controls their avatar. This means figuring out what the player's inputs are going to be and how they will translate into action in the game world in a way that is seamless and puts the player fully in control. For example, in a boxing game, does the player hit a button to throw a punch or maybe use the joystick to simulate moving their fist back and forward? Or maybe some other option, like having to move the avatar while also pressing buttons to pick between a high punch and a low punch? Which will feel better to the player and why?

We can illustrate some difficulties with game control specifically by looking at the variety of decisions that need to be made about how a player's input translates into actions in the game.

In action games, for example, there is the input mapping problem. Players use a gamepad or a similar controller, but in a typical game, there are many more actions available than inputs on the controller. In that case, we will be faced with some tough choices about how to map from the player's physical actions to in-game actions. In a fighting game, we may need to figure out:

- Which buttons/inputs are best for which actions and why? What is it about their positioning and sensitivity that makes them better or worse fit for specific actions? (For example: when to use thumb buttons versus shoulder buttons versus pressing on the analog joysticks, and so on)
- Do we use digital buttons that can only be on or off, or analog joysticks that give us a continuous measurement? Which game actions benefit from analog vs digital?
- Should we use chords? (e.g., $A + down$ for a low kick, $A + up$ for high kick)
- Should we use combos? (e.g., *A–B–A* buttons in sequence for a triple kick)
- Should we use timed actions? (e.g., press and hold the *A* button to "wind up" a forceful kick)

There are no clear answers here, and designers must analyze the controllers that players use and find the best physical inputs for the various types of actions. Players will also come to a game with prior expectations from other games in the genre or from console standards, which need to be respected.

Once we get past input mapping, we need to consider what the input does—for example, how pressing buttons or joystick position moves Mario through a level. Here we worry not just about the choice of inputs but also about what kind of in-game reaction that generates. The following stereotypical examples will highlight the huge variety of choices.

In platformers like *Super Mario Bros.*, pressing left or right buttons moves the avatar by setting *continuous velocity* while the buttons are pressed and resetting to zero when released. Some games, such as *Donkey Kong Jr.*, do it instantaneously, and *Super Mario* appears to change velocity with a very slight ramp up or down, which feels very responsive. Jumping also happens with the push of a button, but in comparison, jump is a *one-shot impulse*—it produces vertical force but only during a very short period of time after the button is pressed.

In games like *Asteroids*, pressing rotate buttons rotates the ship by setting continuous *rotational velocity*. However, pressing the forward or backward buttons sets thrust, or *forward acceleration*, not velocity. The spaceship will slowly gain or lose velocity over time as the player accelerates or decelerates. This makes the spaceship difficult to control and deliberately so.

In modern PC first-person shooters, so-called *mouselook* means that when the player moves their mouse it controls what the character will

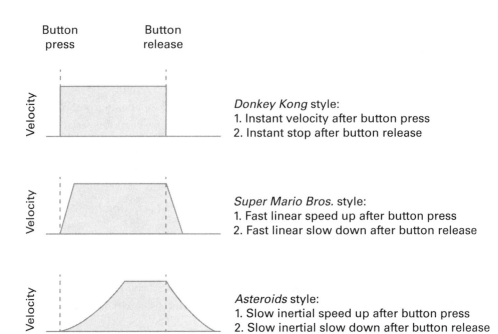

**Figure 3.4**
Examples of how character velocity changes based on button press timings, patterned after Swink (2009)

be looking at. In other words, moving the mouse changes the *rotational position* of the player's camera. In console shooters, however, players do not have a positional mouse, just analog sticks with limited sensitivity, so stick position typically maps to *rotational velocity* instead. Unfortunately, controlling camera via velocity is slower and less accurate than controlling position directly, so console games tend to compensate in some ways, such as by using *autolook* and *autoaim*.

These control mechanics are sometimes called *game feel* mechanics (Swink 2009), since they focus on how player input produces in-game actions, and how their ease or difficulty feels to the player. See the "Further Reading" section for more resources on this topic.

**Progression Mechanics**

Another question we should consider is one of feedback—how will the player know how well they are doing? When playing *Asteroids*, the answer is easy. Each successful hit increases the player's score, and new levels come with more asteroids and more enemy starships to blow up, which gives the player immediate feedback on how far they have gotten.

But in some games this question is harder to answer. In *go* or *chess*, players may not know exactly how they are doing until the endgame is at hand. Given this, players will try to use various approximations, such as counting how many pieces they have left and what positions they occupy and converting that into a numerical score.

*Progression mechanics* are the rules and elements for giving the player feedback on how well they are doing and how they are progressing, hence the name. There is a useful distinction between *direct* and *indirect progression* mechanics.

- *Direct progression* mechanics show the player directly how well they are doing. Often this involves creating some overt metric that is tied to a player's performance and displaying it. Here are some examples of traditional ones:

  - *Score points* or *experience points* (XP), which is just a number that increases as the player accomplishes various actions in the game, shoots enemies, and so on

  - *Levels*, which are earned for reaching specific experience milestones

  - *Achievements*, which are earned for reaching specific, typically uncommon goals

  - *Leaderboards*, which show how players' scores stack up against each other

- *Indirect progression* mechanics change up the game in response to the player's progression. Very often this can be shown via environmental changes. In an action RPG like *Diablo*, as you progress through the game, you discover new territories that look very different, encounter new enemies, or pick up increasingly better loot. Another example might be growing the player's action space in response to their progress. In a life sim game like *The Sims*, the sense of "doing well" is told through the changing material situation of the family (being able to afford better furniture, moving to a larger house, or ultimately not having to work at all). Additionally, many aspects of the game can be treated by players as proxies for how well they are doing in the game and take on the role of progression mechanics as well. For example, "how much money do I have" or "how large is my army" are easy for the player to treat as proxies for progress.

Whether direct or indirect, progression mechanics provide important feedback to the player on how well they are doing, and they also encourage the player to keep playing. Scores and levels can be used to unlock more content or items in the game, giving the player something to look forward to next. Unfolding story can also drive the player to play more to see how it develops. Leaderboards and achievements can appeal to their competitive and completionist natures, respectively.

The motivational aspect of progression mechanics can sometimes seem manipulative, especially when they are obvious and overt, but it is hard to imagine a game that keeps being interesting without giving the player any feedback on how they are doing. So, it is standard practice to have some and to try to make them fit the context and theme of the game, otherwise players will try to infer progression via proxy which might not be best for their experience.

---

**Gamification** is a recent term used to describe using various kinds of progression mechanics to drive behavior outside of games. For example, the Q&A website Stack Overflow gives out XP and achievements to users who are recognized by the community as helpful, which unlocks some new abilities around posting and moderation, and Facebook and Twitter let people vote on their friends' posts with "likes," "favorites," and "shares." These products are attempting to use gamelike mechanics in order to drive people to engage more with the product. However, just having progression mechanics does not by itself motivate the player. It can merely act to strengthen already existing motivation.

And so, gamification is precariously balanced. It can easily fail when the player is not already motivated to participate in the activity in the first place. Progression mechanics only give the player information about how they are doing, but if the activity is not interesting in the first place, they will not be able to make it interesting. We will have more to say about player motivation in chapter 6, "Macrostructure."

---

### Uncertainty Mechanics

Games rely heavily on uncertainty. The outcome of a game depends on many factors that tend to be hard to predict, and the player aims to control this uncertainty via prediction, analysis, or training. In a pure gambling game like *roulette*, the outcome is down to pure luck of the random number generator, which can be analyzed statistically. But in a game like *poker*, there is some uncertainty from randomness, but also some from strategy and psychology. Then in a game like *chess* there is zero randomness, yet it challenges players' mental abilities to the point where their outcome will feel very uncertain. Finally, a physical sport similarly challenges players with uncertain outcomes, but the uncertainty is based on their physical abilities instead.

*Uncertainty mechanics* are the techniques and solutions for adding interesting uncertainty to games. They have been explored in great detail by Costikyan (2013), since they are fundamental across many game genres. Understanding sources of uncertainty and overcoming their effects is an important part of mastery in many kinds of games.

Here we mention a few of the popular types of uncertainty mechanics, and more sources of uncertainty will be discussed in chapter 5, "Gameplay."

*Randomness*, such as numbers produced by physical dice or computer PRNG (pseudorandom number generator) algorithms. These are the kinds of mechanics that involve random values with a specific distribution. For example, a six-sided die will produce values in the set { 1, 2, 3, 4, 5, 6 } with equal probability each time. Random values are very often used to drive many elements of gameplay, from children's board games, where you roll the dice to know how far to move your pawn, to complex war games where various random number generators simulate the uncertain outcomes of military actions. When we roll dice, previous rolls do not affect future rolls in any way. When probabilities remain unchanged from one random result to the next, we call these *stationary* random processes. However, even though they are stationary, that does not mean that the probabilities are the same. A single fair die will have a *uniform* distribution (all probabilities are equal), but this is no longer the case when rolling multiple dice and adding the results. For example, children learn intuitively when playing *Monopoly*, that if they roll two dice they are more likely to roll a seven, and unlikely to roll two or twelve, even though they know nothing about the central limit theorem.

*Shuffling*, such as physical cards or a virtual card deck or set of objects. This is very common in physical games such as card games, as well as in computer games. A shuffled deck is a randomness generator, but the probability of each random value changes over time based on the values already

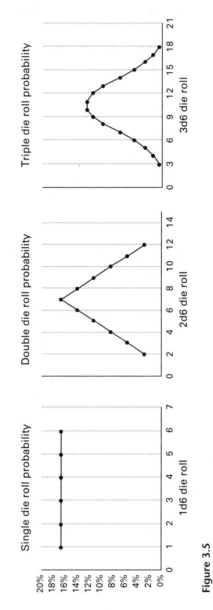

**Figure 3.5**

Result probabilities for a single six-sided die (1d6) and for a sum of two or three six-sided dice (2d6, 3d6)

produced. For example, when we draw from a shuffled deck, the probability of drawing an ace of spades is initially 1/52. However, if we keep drawing cards and we have not drawn the ace, the probability of drawing it next increases. Similarly, once we draw the ace of spades, the probability of drawing it next falls to zero for all subsequent draws. Since each generated value can change the probability of the next one, we call this a *nonstationary* process. Also, the implementation does not have to be as simple as a deck of cards. For example, to prevent losing streaks, which can frustrate the player, we could use a "smart" pseudorandom algorithm that tracks recently produced values and changes probabilities in response.

Figuring out how random generators behave and using them to one's advantage is one of the basic forms of fun in games. For stationary processes, players are challenged to figure out the probability distributions of the various random processes. For example, what are the possible values it produces, whether it is a uniform distribution like a single die or a normal distribution like rolling multiple dice (or perhaps something different still), and, most importantly, how this knowledge can be used for the player's benefit.

Nonstationary processes are even trickier. The player will be challenged to try to predict the next value, which requires figuring out how the distribution changes over time, as well as remembering previous values. However, this kind of challenge can also be very useful. When experienced card players learn to "count cards," for example, they gain an enormous advantage over less sophisticated opponents.

### Resource Management Mechanics

The final common family of mechanics concerns what resources the player has at their disposal to win the game and how they can be improved or exchanged for the player's benefit. For example, the player might control units in the game—armies or vehicles or spaceships or maybe individual people, such as in role-playing games. The player could also own tangible resources like money or raw materials to buy things, produce items, and so on—perhaps even owning factories or cities or entire planets, depending entirely on the game.

We will use the name *resources* to denote the things we can acquire and use to accomplish our goals in the game. Combined with rules for how they can be managed, these form the *resource management mechanics* family. Let's look at the variety we could consider.

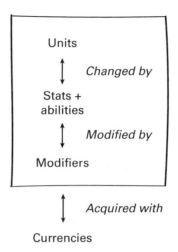

**Figure 3.6**
Relationships between different resource management elements

*Units*. There are items in the game world that the player directs, manages, or encounters. Units that have specific abilities are a common resource mechanic. Game pieces in *chess* or *checkers* are examples of units, as are properties in *Monopoly*. In computer games, even very early games like *Space Invaders* already had a variety of enemy units with different behaviors.

Unit mechanics reflect questions such as:

- What are the units in the game and how are they controlled by the player or AI?
- How do those units act? What are their abilities?
- How can those abilities change or be strategically improved?

Every game has its own unique design for units. However, games in specific genres often tend to cluster around common patterns.

- *Classic war games* have units that correspond to real-world military units with similar movement and combat characteristics, such as some notion of firing range or movement range based on terrain.
- *Real-time strategy games* like *StarCraft* have a variety of unit types with strongly differentiated abilities, interlocking so that players need a team of units that support each other. A global tech tree may unlock new unit types as the game progresses.

- *Role-playing games* typically have fewer, more complex units. They are the characters that live in the game world, and they might have richer backstories, stats, and extensive abilities which get acquired as the game progresses.
- *Management games* may have a variety of units that consume and produce specific combinations of resources, and they may even be unmovable (like buildings in *SimCity* or cities in *Civilization*). The choice of what to build given the player's abilities and future threats presents trade-offs.
- Some games have unexpected units. For example, the player's stable of cars in driving games like *Forza* form a collection of units with different abilities.

The choice of units is going to very strongly describe what the game is about, and what kind of gameplay it will produce.

Genres also evolve typical ways for how those units will be controlled. Since the player usually has to deal with multiple units at once, UI issues become important, like how the player selects units, groups units together, issues commands, inspects their state, and so on.

*Abilities.* We have mentioned abilities in passing. They are the types of actions that units can perform. Some games keep the ability vocabulary limited. In *checkers*, each game piece follows very simple rules. But other games delight in introducing a zoo of units and abilities, such as role-playing games with complicated magic systems, or card games with card-specific abilities.

The more abilities units can have, the more it opens up the player's action space and challenges the player's ability to pick the best action. Complexity does not arise just from their number, it can also arise from their variety and how they interlock with each other, such as in *chess*, where a few, highly differentiated abilities produce a very large game state space.

In some games, it is also possible to change or improve abilities over time, which can be used to present the player with interesting challenges. For example, consider a player in an action-strategy RTS game who just developed a well-balanced army of attack units, defense units, healer units, and so on. During the game session, they research an upgrade that will make their attack units twice as fast but considerably weaker. This presents a dilemma. Does it make sense to upgrade all attack units? What will that do to the team structure? Does this mean adding more healers or defenders, and is that even affordable? Often there is only one way to figure this out: experiment and see what happens.

Designers differ on where they land on *minimalism* versus *maximalism*. Is it better to have fewer unit types and abilities that are strongly differentiated or more units and abilities with a wide spectrum of subtle trade-offs? This is a very subjective question and will present players with different challenges. On one end, some players relish games that require an encyclopedic knowledge of a large number of units and abilities, and other players enjoy minimalism and sticking to very few rules that combine in complex ways. The right choice will very much depend on the genre, what kind of a player is going to play this game, and what player experience the designer is looking for.

*Stats.* When we design units with different abilities, and especially if we want units to change their abilities over time, we may want to quantify it in some way that is easy for the player to understand (and the computer to calculate).

Numerical stats (such as attack points, health points, and so on) have been a part of games for a long time. Early war games already used attack points, armor points, and movement points to quantify how the different types of vehicles and human groups would behave on the battlefield (Dunnigan 2000). Fantasy RPGs like *Dungeons & Dragons* inherited this approach, along with other war game elements, and described characters using stats such as strength, dexterity, wisdom, and so on. We see echoes of these early data models to this day in RPGs and other genres.

Stats are often used to:

- Modulate probabilities (e.g., higher attack points mean higher chance of winning in combat)
- Modulate abilities (e.g., higher movement points specify how fast a unit can move per turn, a higher attack range means hitting targets further away)
- Unlock abilities (e.g., higher strength lets a fighter equip a secondary weapon with new abilities)

Changing unit abilities (or introducing new units with new abilities) changes up how the player plays the game and forces them to discover new tactics and new strategies for winning. This is typically a good thing. It prevents the player from sticking to a single strategy that works for them.

*Modifiers.* Given a stat such as "strength," players may want to be able to improve this stat and make the unit more powerful. Stat-altering mechanics are commonly called *modifiers*, or *buffs*, or *power-ups*. The idea is to reify the change in stats into a concrete in-game resource that can be acquired and then strategically used by the player to modify their abilities.

Games of all genres are full of stat modifiers.

- In *Mario Kart*, collecting mushrooms gives you an automatic speed boost, and banana peels throw you off your trajectory, both for a short period of time.

- In *Diablo*, magic weapons or clothing will give boosts to various stats of the person wearing it, but there are many restrictions on who can wear what kinds of equipment.

- In *Civilization*, various technologies give a permanent boost to resource production from farms, mines, and other types of land tiles, but they are expensive to acquire.

... And so on.

---

**Buffs.** Improving stats for the player's benefit is often called *buffing* and reducing stats is called *nerfing*. Both buffing and nerfing accomplish the goal of changing up the player's abilities, but they have a different emotional effect. Players prefer to see their units get better and more powerful. It feels like a reward for hard work, and having them nerfed feels like punishment for not doing something right. For this reason, it is generally better to have in-game items and events that buff stats rather than nerf them.

---

Finally, even if a game has stats, being able to modify them is not strictly necessary. Games like *Space Invaders* and *chess* have units with a variety of abilities that do not change most of the time, but those abilities combine together to form challenging gameplay.

*Currencies and items.* We have already talked about units and their abilities and stats. Units in a game are a kind of resources, but there are other types as well.

- *Money and other currencies,* which you can use to buy other resources and perhaps gain by selling resources or as rewards for progressing through the game

- *Items* that can be used, such as weapons in war games, or clothing and spell books in RPGs; you can store items in an inventory or potentially equip them on your units
- *Consumables*, such as fuel for your tanks or food for your soldiers, which will be consumed in the process of buffing or enabling some other elements
- *Raw resources*, such as crafting items, which are not usable directly but can be used to create other units (like using steel to build tanks) or to craft items (like turning iron and coal into steel)
- *Space* itself can be a resource, such as in *Risk* where the terrain you occupy produces a certain yield of other resources per unit time.

These kinds of resources are intended to be gained, exchanged, and perhaps consumed—and, ideally, they will interlock with each other and with other mechanics and create an in-game economy. We will come back to economies, currencies, and crafting in the next chapter when we talk about game systems.

### Beyond the Four Families

In this section we discussed four popular families of mechanics: control, progression, uncertainty, and resource management. These are used across a variety of games and genres, which makes them perfect for an initial introduction.

However, there are many more mechanics than these. For example, each genre typically makes use of its own unique mechanics or those shared with similar genres. The mechanics of a racing game are going to be different from a turn-based strategy game and different still from a real-time first-person shooter.

For more information about specialized mechanics, it is best to turn to specialized texts that focus on specific genres. See the "Further Reading" section for more pointers on some popular ones.

### Mechanics Design

When we create a new game, we will rarely create brand new mechanics that have never been seen before. More likely, we will revisit existing mechanics and maybe invent some variants or remix them and put them together in novel ways (and even that can be a tough design challenge). This is a context-specific design problem, but, fortunately, there are a few generic *heuristics* for how we could improve mechanics in general across a variety of game types.

### Design Heuristics

In his book *The Aesthetic of Play*, Upton offers six useful heuristics for how we can evaluate and improve game mechanics (2015).[5] The heuristics are:

**Choice.** *Player should perceive a range of possible actions.* Players will have an immediate reaction to their perceived action space. If it is too narrow or constraining, they will get bored doing the same thing over and over again. However, if it offers too many choices, they may get confused and frustrated. The ideal size of the perceived action space is important to get right, and it is going to depend on the audience, game type, player expectations, and so on (for example, compare expectations for a children's game like *Snakes and Ladders* to a sophisticated game like *Magic the Gathering*). In practice, a simple rule of thumb is that games with more choices will often feel richer and more open than variants with fewer choices.

**Variety.** *Actions are not repeated.* Actions should be numerous, but it feels interesting to have the available actions change over time compared to choosing from the same actions over and over. When new actions suddenly become available or our favorite ones become unavailable, or when we get a whole new set of abilities we did not have before, it immediately grabs the player's attention. It forces the player out of a comfortable rut and into actively evaluating their new situation. This is especially important because players will actively learn how to use existing mechanics to their advantage, so having the same unchanging mechanics will make it easier to master them, which in turn will make them feel uninteresting and "played out." Changing the set of mechanics over time is a good way to keep the player actively learning.

**Consequence.** *Actions have outcomes.* The decision to do or not do something should have a consequence that the player can attribute to their

---

5. Although Upton speaks of them in terms of action and intent horizons, we adapt them using the vocabulary we have been developing so far in this text.

decision. If the player's actions have no consequences (for example, whatever is destined to happen will happen), the player will lose the feeling of agency or control over their situation. And if the player's actions have a consequence that cannot be attributed (such as when the outcomes happen much later), it will prevent them from understanding how the game universe works. Mastering consequence and causality in the game world is necessary for forming successful long-term plans and strategies. It is interesting for the player to figure out which actions have the best consequences and juggle multiple opportunities whose consequences conflict with each other (such as the choice between short-term or long-term gains).

**Predictability.** *Outcomes can be anticipated.* Assuming that actions have outcomes, a player should be able to learn to anticipate those outcomes at least to some degree. Being able to make theories about how the world works is at the heart of being able to make long-term plans. For example, if combat mechanics do not behave predictably enough, the player may have a hard time understanding how combat works in the game and grow immensely frustrated. Complete predictability and unpredictability are both undesirable—the most interesting mechanics lie somewhere in the middle. The player should be able to figure out how the various mechanics work with enough effort, and then make use of them.

**Uncertainty.** *Outcomes are not predetermined.* This is the flip side of predictability. A fully predetermined outcome is a problem, just like a fully unpredictable one is. The game benefits from a degree of understandable uncertainty, which the player may try to master. One common source of uncertainty are randomness generators, such as dice or decks of cards. However, a more popular source is other players because they are far more interesting, understandable, and unpredictable than simple dice or cards. Even in purely deterministic games such as *chess*, the presence of the other player fills each game moment with rich uncertainty.

**Satisfaction.** *Desirable outcomes are attainable.* The focus here is on the likelihood and work required to produce desirable outcomes, such as advancing or winning. If a game is completely unwinnable, if the player keeps failing and failing at what they do, they will get frustrated and lose interest. Overwhelming difficulty is a common source of this kind of frustration. At the same time, if the game always delivers desirable outcomes, if the player always gets what they want, this is not going to be interesting, either. We need to strike a good balance between challenging the player in interesting ways yet making it possible for them to reach their goals.

These heuristics are useful because they point out some general principles behind what makes mechanics interesting and engaging for players. We can keep them in the back of the mind as we seek to design new game elements and actions ourselves.

### Primary and Derived Mechanics

Beyond designing the elements and actions of the game, we should also consider that players will generate their own abstractions on top of the ones we provide as they learn to master the game. For example, when we learn how to play *chess*, we learn about the pieces, the actions, and the rules of the game. We learn how to move the queen or the rook, we learn that pawns advance one or two tiles forward but attack on the diagonal, and so on.

But in order to play it *well*, we need to figure out a slightly different set of abstractions. We need to learn the concept of protecting the king and how to gain control over the game board, what it means to sacrifice, how to fork, or how to pin. We may want to learn about endgames and acquire an encyclopedic knowledge of standard openings. And this is by no means limited to *chess*—competitive *Hearthstone* players have their vocabulary of decks and deck types, MMO players talk a lot about tactics for dealing with various mobs, and so on.

This is the difference between primary mechanics and derived ones. *Primary mechanics* are what is required to play the game. They define the gameplay. *Derived mechanics*, on the other hand, are player abstractions that have been created and defined by the community of players, usually distilling extensive experience playing the game and noticing additional patterns. In some games, they may also be called *standard tactics* or, less often, *second-order mechanics*.[6]

---

6. This usage of terms "first order" and "second order" mechanics is present in the *Characteristics of Games* book (Elias, Garfield and Gutschera 2012) and "Formal Abstract Design Tools" (Church 1999), among others. However, cardinal ordering only invites questions we do not know how to answer. For example, if we have first and second, what could be third-order mechanics? Instead of pursuing this further, we will only differentiate between primary mechanics and all other ones.

This kind of expert mental modeling is not limited to games. Experts in all sorts of areas will commonly identify patterns and structures that occur repeatedly. Derived mechanics are not required to play, but they are very useful since they encode expert knowledge about how the game is structured beyond the obvious ways.

As designers, we are not obligated to design or predict derived mechanics. We may not even know what they are until the player community discovers them. However, as we design and playtest the game, we need to be on a lookout for them in case players discover some mechanics that make the game too easy to figure out or otherwise not enjoyable.

### Summary

In this chapter we explored the beginnings of the design process. The key takeaways are:

- *Mechanics* are the basic building blocks of games. They are idiomatic combinations of smaller components, such as game pieces, player actions, and rules that govern how they interact. Many different types of mechanics exist, but in this text, we only describe four families.

  - *Control mechanics*, relating to controlling one's avatar in the game world

  - *Progression mechanics*, relating to understanding and controlling one's advancement in the game

  - *Uncertainty mechanics*, relating to trying to understand and predict an uncertain future

  - *Resource management mechanics*, relating to treating elements of the game as resources that can be managed and manipulated in specific ways

- We sometimes also see games being described in terms of their "nouns and verbs," which is a linguistic metaphor for thinking about mechanics.

- Games are *stateful*, and as players interact with a game, the state of the game changes. How a game unfolds over time can be analyzed in terms of the trajectory over its possible *state space*. Similarly, the player's set of available actions can be represented as an *action space*, and the player's perception of this space is hugely important.

- As we design the specific mechanics for our games, we can use the *Upton heuristics* to help us evaluate how they will interact with the player and with each other.

- Finally, we should expect that players may discover new ways to use the pieces, actions, and rules that we created, extending our intended set of mechanics in different and unexpected ways.

Coming up next, in chapter 4, "Systems," we will examine how those mechanics in turn come together to form larger systems before turning our attention to gameplay in the chapters that follow.

## Further Reading

### History of Mechanics

The concepts of *game mechanics* and *dynamics* date back at least to the Cold War–era research communities that used games as research and education tools (rather than entertainment experiences), for example, to simulate military conflicts or for teaching about complex systems such as businesses or population behavior. Materials from that era already use these terms in ways that we recognize today, even if not exactly the same: "mechanics" as combinations of game rules plus additional elements (Greenlaw, Herron, and Rawdon 1962, 149–150), and "dynamics" as the behavior of the game and the way it unfolds over time (Abt et al. 1965, 43–44; Adams 1970).

In entertainment, the concept of *mechanics* seems to have been first adopted by war-gaming enthusiasts, as the term appears to be already in use in war-gaming design in the early 1970s. Then with the advent of video games as a mass market phenomenon, we start to see the term being used more broadly both by video game developers as well as growing enthusiast press.[7] By the mid-1990s mechanics become a more common term as can be seen in various proceedings from the Game Developers Conference or

---

7. In war-gaming, the term appears in *The Avalon Hill General* as early as 1971 (Avalon Hill, Inc. 1971, 3). In video games, the printed manuals for the games *Archon* (Westfall 1983) and *Batalyx* (Llamasoft 1985) mention the "mechanics" of those games in passing, suggesting the term was already used in game design. On the enthusiast press side, the *Electronic Games* magazine in the early 1980s is perhaps the first to have used "mechanics" in reviewing gameplay of various arcade and home console games.

articles in the *Game Developer Magazine,* and in game reviews in popular press.

Perhaps because this term has such a long history and crosses a number of communities, there is no single and clear definition of mechanics. The importance of rules is almost always at the forefront—for example, Brathwaite and Schreiber (2009, 28) describe mechanics as "another term for what others might commonly call a 'rule.'" But beyond that, various communities tend to emphasize different aspects of mechanics (see "Defining Game Mechanics" (Sicart 2008) for a survey of other definitions), and it is not unusual for designers from different backgrounds to approach this topic with different assumptions. Fortunately, these slight semantic differences do not seem to have a noticeable negative impact on design practice.

In this text, the usage of the term *mechanics* is based on contemporary use in video game design specifically and closely matches that of (Sellers 2017, 101) who defines them as "semantically viable (that is, meaningful) combinations of tokens and rules."

### Taxonomies

There have also been a few attempts at compiling standard taxonomies of mechanics; however, they have not been adopted in industry practice so far.

- *Patterns in Game Design* (Bjork and Holopainen 2004) is a treatment of patterns in the style of "software patterns," including a number of game mechanics. Unfortunately, the book is currently out of print.

- "The 400 Project" by Hal Barwood and Noah Falstein is an abandoned project to document 400 rules of game design that might be of historical interest (Barwood and Falstein n.d.).

### In-depth Explorations

Numerous designers have discussed specific types or families of mechanics from their own perspective in that design space. Some of the great resources along these lines include:

- *The Aesthetic of Play* (Upton 2015), especially chapters 3 and 4 which discuss players' action spaces, the distinction between actual and perceived actions, and the heuristics for designing them.

- *Game Feel* (Swink 2009) contains a highly detailed examination of action mechanics including the analyses of input/output timings and the variations in affordances of different kinds of input devices.

- *Uncertainty in Games* (Costikyan 2013) provides a thorough examination of types of uncertainty and how they are employed using many examples from existing games.
- *Characteristics of Games* (Elias, Garfield and Gutschera 2012) is highly recommended for details on multiplayer mechanics including a large variety of decision points for designers especially of board and card games. Related, *The Kobold Guide to Board Game Design* (Selinker 2011) brings together various board game designers to share insights into several specific board game mechanics.
- *Advanced Game Design* (Sellers 2017) goes into great depth on the topic of units, resources, currencies, and setting up economies and systems in which they participate.
- *Wargames Handbook* (Dunnigan 2000) is a great resource for a history of unit and resource mechanics in the context of board war games.

In addition, the *GDC Vault* is a great repository of talks from practicing designers discussing their work at the annual *Game Developers Conference*. These talks can be a great source of knowledge about design details from a wide variety of games and genres. Slides and videos can be found at http://gdcvault.com.

## Individual Exercises

### 3.1. Mechanics
Pick a board or video game you know well. Describe three different mechanics in that game. For each of those mechanics, describe how it works in terms of the objects and actions involved, and the rules that govern this specific mechanic.

### 3.2. State Spaces and Action Spaces
Pick a board game you know well.

a. Describe what information goes into completely describing the state of the game at a point in time (e.g., positions of all game pieces, and so on). Is this a fully or partially observable state space?
b. Consider the actions that the player can take. Does the number and type of actions change over time as the game progresses from the beginning to the end? How does this affect the feel of the game?

### 3.3. Implicit and Explicit Mechanics
Consider a computer game that you like. List some of the implicit mechanics that the player only learns over time or learns by playing. Now consider what would happen if you made the player aware of these mechanics right from the beginning—how would that change their experience?

### 3.4. Control Mechanics

Consider some favorite action video game, one played with a console controller. List the various actions the player can do and how they are mapped to controller buttons or directional joysticks.

Why do you think the developer decided on this particular mapping of actions to inputs? Is there something about some buttons that makes them better suited for particular actions? Also, is this mapping conventional compared to other games of this type?

### 3.5. Progression Mechanics

Pick a game you like. What kind of progression mechanics does it use to give the player feedback on their progression in the game? Are these mechanics successful in bringing players back to the game and to keep playing it?

### 3.6. Resource Management

Pick some game you are familiar with. Describe at least three different unit types in the game and how they are differentiated from each other. Do stats or abilities play a role in making the units different?

## Group Exercises

### G3.1. Design Challenge: Changing the Mechanics of *Checkers*

In this exercise we will explore making changes to the mechanics of *checkers* and observing how they impact the player's experience.

a. Play several rounds of *checkers* to remind yourself of gameplay. Then, pick some mechanics in the game and change them in some way that you feel is interesting and unusual, for example:

- You could add or modify rules about existing game pieces and actions. (For example, what if each player started with a "king" piece that they already own?)

- You could also add new pieces and new rules that govern them. (For example, you can invent a new piece that has a different behavior from the existing "pawn" and "king" pieces.)

- You could also remove mechanics, although checkers is already minimal enough that there is not much left to remove.

b. Discuss how you think these changes will affect your gameplay experience.

c. Play several rounds with the new mechanics in place and observe your experience. Consider especially the following elements:

- Speed. Is it faster or slower, and why?

- Challenge. Is it harder or easier, and why?

- Appeal. Is it more enjoyable or less, and why?

To complete the exercise, describe the following:

d. In detail, describe the new mechanics, including the actions, pieces, and rules that are affected.

e. Describe how this change in mechanics affected your experience of playing the game, how you *expected* these changes to affect your experience, and how what effect you *observed*. How does it feel to play the game now as opposed to playing with the original rules?

**G3.2. Design Challenge: Remixing Unrelated Mechanics into *Checkers***
In this exercise we will consider what would happen if we added some unexpected mechanics into *checkers*.

a. Play several rounds of *checkers* to remind yourself of gameplay. Then, add some unexpected, unrelated mechanic by drawing inspiration from one of the generic types we discussed in this chapter.

   • *Progression mechanics*, like points, scores, etc.
   • *Uncertainty mechanics*, like dice or random cards
   • *Resource management mechanics*, like adding stats or abilities

   Some examples: you could add uncertainty by making piece capture require a die roll, you could add attack and health points and have capture only succeed after health falls down to zero, and so on.

b. Discuss how you think these changes will affect your gameplay experience.

c. Play several rounds with the new mechanics in place. Observe your experience and pay attention to whether this variant feels more or less appealing or enjoyable than original.

   To complete the exercise, describe the following:

d. In detail, describe the new mechanics, including the actions, pieces, and rules that are affected.

e. Describe *how* this change in mechanics affected your experience of playing the game, how you expected your experience to change, and what you observed.

f. Analyze *why* you think your changes to mechanics brought about this change in experience. What is it about your changes that had this effect?

# 4  Systems

In the previous chapter, we talked about mechanics and listed some types of mechanics with their examples. Now we can turn to discussing how mechanics work together and how they can be analyzed as dynamic systems which encapsulate a variety of mechanics and their interactions.

First, we will look at how mechanics chain together into sequences of relationships such as producers and consumers and how to analyze them. Second, we look at what happens once chains themselves start interlocking and feeding back into themselves and each other. Finally, we will look at how these kinds of dynamic systems can be composed when making a new game. But first, an example.

## Motivating Example: *Diablo*

*Diablo III* is an action RPG in a style sometimes described as a "dungeon crawler." The game is set in a perilous fantasy world where the story will ask us to explore its many mysterious dungeons, ruins, and secret areas, and deal with the hordes of monsters and enemy forces that occupy them.

The gameplay is oriented around a repeating "explore, fight, and return" pattern. With a motley crew of adventurers under our control, we leave camp to find the next dungeon filled with monsters and hidden treasure. The team goes through and clears out each area, and they pick up items dropped by monsters and loot treasure from hidden chests. Eventually their backpacks get full, so everybody gathers their things and heads back to camp to sell the loot and recuperate, regain some health, maybe craft some potions or fix weapons or train up on new spells. Then it is time to venture out again.

**Figure 4.1**
Screenshot from *Diablo III*

This simplified example shows a number of mechanics that interlock together. We can talk about them as if composed of several high-level systems, such as:

**Inventory**

- We gain items from fighting (weapons, treasure, crafting resources, etc.).
- Weapons can be equipped on characters on the team.
- Other items can be put in inventory or left behind.
- Inventory is finite, and initially small, but it can be upgraded.
- Back in camp, items from inventory can be sold, or inventory can be emptied to storage.

**Economy**

- We gain items from fighting (weapons, treasure, crafting resources, etc.).
- Back in camp, we can sell items to gain gold.
- We can then spend gold in different ways:
  - To buy different items (weapons, potions, spells, etc.)
  - To buff stats or items (e.g., upgrading inventory size)
  - On services (learn a new spell, get a weapon fixed, etc.)

## Crafting

- We gain items from fighting (weapons, treasure, crafting resources, etc.).
- We can use crafting resources at a crafting station to make new kinds of items.
- Some items may be also "disassembled" back into crafting resources.
- Crafting requires a recipe, listing how resources combine and their proportions.
- Crafting recipes are themselves items that be bought, sold, found, etc.

... And so on.

This is just a quick illustration of three different *game systems:* inventory, economy, and crafting. At this point we omit combat, exploration, and several other systems present in these games and concentrate on just those three to make the discussion simpler—but there are certainly more systems in *Diablo* than those three.

One interesting aspect of these systems, which we will come back to, is that they are designed to *interlock.* They share various mechanics (such as items or currencies) but use them for very different purposes. Interlocking systems become more interesting as we discuss below.

## Game Systems

We can consider a system as a *collection of mechanics set up to work together* in specific ways. The combination of which elements are used and how they are arranged together defines the system's performance.

Three examples of systems were mentioned above.

- Inventory: item equipping, ownership, and carrying limits
- Economy: the exchange of resources, items, and currencies
- Crafting: the transformation of some resources and items into others

Systems are made up of mechanics. To make those systems interact with each other, they should *share mechanics* but for different purposes. In our example, inventory interacts with economy via items (they can be carried in the inventory but also bought and sold), and both also interact with crafting via crafting materials (those can also be carried, bought, sold). Shared mechanics create interactions and trade-offs between systems and force the player to make interesting decisions.

Because they interlock like that, a player who comes across a new item will be faced with the interesting problem of having to evaluate it in context of the various systems and their trade-offs. For example, is this item useful for crafting? Can I sell it later, and is it worth it? Is there enough capacity in the inventory? Do I have enough strength to carry it all? A broad mechanic like items or currencies can often interact with *many* systems, including ones we have not talked about such as combat.

### Setting and Systems

Systems are a very useful abstraction. When we try to come up with the design for a new game, we can start from mechanics. However, sometimes it is more fruitful to start the conversation on the level of entire game systems instead because that lets us "paint with a larger brush" as it were, to start at a higher level before we come back to fill in the details. Some designers like Sellers go even further and suggest that systems are the *most important* abstraction level for games because systems-based interaction is what makes games unique compared to other types of entertainment.

When designing a new game, the choice of "setting and systems" is often a good starting point. What is the setting where the game takes place, and what are the systems that the player will interact with? Answering these questions first will help push the design in a specific direction, and simplify the process. For example, we could decide to focus on "a fantasy setting with combat, exploration, weapons, and random dungeons," and that starts us in the direction of *Diablo*. Or perhaps we focus on "a historical game with economy, military conquest, and country management," which pushes the design along a strategy direction like *Civilization*. We do not specify all the details just yet, but these commitments are already enough to get us started so that they can be fleshed out with specific mechanics.

---

**Code systems.** The word *system* is also often used in a different context: to describe stand-alone programming modules, such as the physics system or the graphics system. These kind of *code systems* are not collection of mechanics, although mechanics such as "gravity gun" can be built on top of them. It is usually clear from context when people talk about code systems or gameplay systems.

## Layering

A more developed game will typically contain a multitude of systems that interlock in interesting ways, like gears in a watch. For an extreme example, here is an incomplete list of systems that can be found in a strategy game like *Civilization V*.

- Geography: a random map full of resources that feed other systems
- Territory: tiles owned by players and which produce resources for their owner
- Cities: unmovable units that produce other units, and gather resources from surrounding tiles
- Buildings: smaller units built inside cities, that generate resources or currency, convert resources, and so on
- Armies and Combat: movable units that explore, attack, improve resources on tiles, and so on
- Neighboring Civilizations: AIs that compete with the player
- Trading and Diplomacy: exchanging agreements or resources with neighbors, starting and ending wars
- Economy: using currency to buy or upgrade units, tiles, etc.
- Science: tech tree that unlocks better units and buildings, reveals new tiles, and so on
- Culture and Golden Ages: systems for unlocking large-scale buffs
- Religion: passive resource generation that requires a large base of converted cities
- Victory Paths: several different chains of demanding requirements, whoever satisfies any of the chains first wins the game

… and a number of additional ones.

This list is not intended to be exhaustive but to give some examples of how different systems can work in one game.

The list also does not mention how the systems interlock, but they commonly do. For example, natural resources such as wheat or coal are a shared mechanic that provides interactions. Map tiles contain random natural resources (geography), and if we can gain control over those tiles (territory), we could extract them or convert to other resources (via buildings). Those other resources in turn we can use to grow the population (in cities) and build an army so we can attack our enemies (combat).

Finding the right layering of systems and interlocks is a difficult, game-specific design problem, and it is often done by starting small and getting some base systems right, then growing the design from there. Sometimes this can be done descriptively, "on paper," but it is beneficial to implement simplified *system prototypes* as part of the design process to know how they behave in the real world when actual players start using them.

### Thinking in Systems

Game systems are a kind of an abstraction that elides the details of the individual mechanics when they are not needed and allows us to focus on how the whole game is put together from larger pieces.

Systems are common in other areas of design as well as in science and engineering. For example, in automotive design one could talk about the transmission or the engine as if they were standalone entities and how they interact with each other, and then only worry about the implementation details once necessary. For another example, in biology and medicine we can talk about systems of different kinds of organs and tissues working in concert, such as the nervous system, only worrying about the lower-level workings when needed.

In game design, there are three specific benefits.

1. *Isolation:* It is easier to discuss how some mechanics work together if we focus on just them in separation from the outside (as we will when we discuss feedback loops below).

2. *Reuse:* Existing systems are solutions to particular design problems, and we can sometimes apply those solutions to our problems or draw inspiration from them for our own games (for example, a game with a successful crafting system can inspire similar designs in others).

3. *Scaling:* It is easier to discuss large-scale gameplay elements like pacing or progression when our building blocks are large (we get to these later in this chapter).

A working designer needs to have a breadth of experience with a variety of existing systems and a multitude of prior examples to draw on. When faced with a design problem, they will be able to lean on their experience with other games with different types of systems, different implementations and pros and cons, to find a good solution.

## Mechanic Chains and Loops

We often find that mechanics end up forming *chains of interactions*, and often those chains form a *loop*, such as conversion loops or feedback loops. Chaining and looping are common, fundamental design patterns, and they can exist within a system or span multiple systems.

We now take a deeper look at how that might work. Continuing with action RPG games like *Diablo*, we will look specifically at the *economy* and *inventory systems*. We will see how resource acquisition and conversion mechanics end up forming a loop, and we will discuss some ways to analyze the behavior of such loops.

### Conversion Chains

Consider our action RPG example from above. Let's say that we find an area overrun by trolls, and trolls carry loot, which can be collected. So, we send our team to fight them, and let's say it plays out like this:

1. The team fights as many trolls as possible. After getting loot from 10 trolls, their inventory is full, so they go back to camp. Also, in total they lost 60 health points and used up 100 arrows, so they need to heal and restock.
2. They sell 10 troll loot items for 10 gold each for a total of +100 gold.
3. They restock ammo for −10 gold and find a healer to restore the lost health points for −60 gold, so they spend a total of −70 gold to get back on their feet so they can go out again.

Note that the net result from the expedition is +30 gold, so they are making a profit.

We can diagram this sequence as seen in figure 4.2.

This is a kind of a *resource diagram*, which shows how resources are produced or consumed by various actions available to the player. The diagram is very coarse, since it omits the details of how much can be converted,

**Figure 4.2**
Example resource diagram

under what circumstances, and so on. In the diagram, we use rectangles to denote what resources are being consumed and produced and then round nodes to denote actions that consume and produce them.

The economy mechanics (selling, healing, restocking) and combat mechanics (fighting to get loot) are set up in a *conversion chain* of producers and consumers. Each step provides something that is an input to the next step. In this example fighting costs some health and ammo and it removes one monster from the game board, but it generates loot. This loot can then be sold for gold, and gold can be used to restore the health and ammo that we spent on the fight.

In other words, this diagram illustrates the *resource conversion* aspect of the troll hunt.

- *Fighting* converts trolls, health, and ammo into loot.
- *Selling* converts loot into gold.
- *Healing* converts gold into health.
- *Restocking* converts gold into ammo.

In this diagram we did not specify *tuning values*, that is, how much of each resource gets consumed or produced, but we mentioned them in the description and noticed that this chain is net profitable. It takes effort to go through each step, but in the process we gain some income (+100 gold, ammo, health, loot), incur some costs (–70 gold, ammo, health, loot), and end up with the net profit of +30 gold.

### Calculating Exchange Rates

We can also turn these tuning values around, and consider our resources in terms of their *exchange rates*, that is, how much one resource is worth in terms of other resources:

- *Selling:* 1 loot item → 10 gold
- *Restocking:* 10 gold → 100 arrows (or 1 gold → 10 arrows)

  therefore, 1 loot item → 100 arrows

- *Healing:* 60 gold → 60 health (or 1 gold → 1 health)

  therefore, 1 loot item → 10 health

- *Fighting:* As described above, an average of 10 loot is gained from attacking 10 monsters and losing 60 health and 100 arrows

  therefore, 1 monster → 1 loot item, –6 health, –10 arrows

- All together: fighting, then selling, restocking, and healing

    1 monster → 1 loot item, −6 health, −10 arrows

    → 1 monster → 10 gold, −6 health, −10 arrows

    → 1 monster → 9 gold, −6 health

    → 1 monster → 3 gold

The last line of this resource conversion analysis shows something interesting: monsters are basically free money. If we find a monster and we are willing to spend the gold (and labor!) to fight it and deal with the consequences, we can generate even more gold. By doing this over and over again, each monster encounter will net us +3 gold pieces on average not counting labor or incidental costs.

## Conversion Loops

Now imagine doing this repeatedly. If we ignore the actual hard work of combat and travel and just focus on the resources being gained and lost, we can represent repeating the chain as a loop that looks like figure 4.3.

The chain repeats itself to form a *loop*, because the outputs of a step eventually loop around, and produce inputs to the same step in the future. The loop as we described it always produces the same amount, but that doesn't have to be the case as we see in a bit.

We mentioned that this loop is *profitable*. Each time through it we lose 70 gold but gain 100 gold, so our income is higher than costs. Therefore, we could keep making more money by doing it more than once. It is easy to imagine what would happen if we went hunting over and over. Our gold inventory over time would look something like figure 4.4.

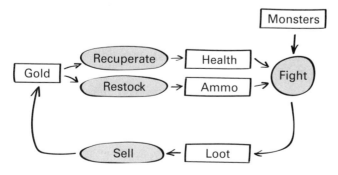

**Figure 4.3**
Resource diagram from figure 4.2, arranged into a loop

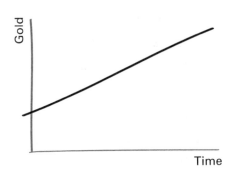

**Figure 4.4**
Gold inventory that increases at a stable rate

This shows a nice linear trend as each iteration generates more in income than we pay in expenses. Over time we could amass quite a bit of gold.

Assuming that trolls were respawned without end, we would have an *infinite source* of gold. But this is bad. Once there is an easy source of infinite income, it can generally be exploited by players and will destroy the carefully tuned challenge and progression on which many games rely. For example, with infinite gold it could become very easy to gain access to expensive and overpowered weapons and armor, which will make the game unchallenging and not fun.

We could remedy this in several ways. One, we could change the *tuning values*, that is, the coefficients of how much different things cost. For example, what if we doubled the cost of health potions and arrows from −7 gold per troll to −14 gold? Then the player's wealth over time would look more like figure 4.5.

This loop now turned *unprofitable*, as the player would lose wealth each time they went through it. If they kept repeating it, the reward for all their hard work would be going bankrupt. This is not desirable, and players would regard it as a *broken* loop.

We need to look at other options. The player should not be able to get resources endlessly or lose them endlessly. If it is desirable for the player to gain resources in a production loop, there needs to be something that stops them from iterating through the loop forever.

Here are some ideas of things we could do:

1. Add a hard cap either on the player (such as a weapon damage mechanic that makes the weapon break after a few attacks) or on the harvested

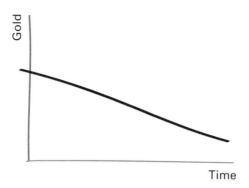

**Figure 4.5**
Gold inventory that decreases at a stable rate

resources (such as limiting the number of trolls). This is a hard stop on the loop after some number of iterations, forcing the player to switch away, which is not the most satisfying option, but it might reflect realistic limits on resource exploitation.

2. Make the outcome less predictable (so the player may have to go back to camp empty-handed). This adds uncertainty, potentially increasing the cost in randomized ways. But an experienced player will be able to figure out the expected reward by averaging the results over many attempts.

3. Increase labor cost of combat or travel (make it not fun to do this too much). This basically adds a cost of going through the conversion loop, but the cost is not in resources; it is something external like time spent on the activity. Spending a lot of time on rote actions to iterate through a resource loop is commonly called *grinding*, and many players have a negative opinion of loops that require it (but will keep doing so even while complaining if the loop is profitable enough).

4. Scale the profit curve over time so that the loop changes from profitable to unprofitable as the player continues to go through it.

This last example is particularly interesting. It is an example of *dynamic tuning*. For example, we can adjust the cost dynamically by raising the prices of ammo and health potions over time. Let's say ammo and health start out costing us −70 gold per trip but then increased by an additional −10 gold with each trip and the gold we get from selling loot remains the same, then the player's gold inventory will look like figure 4.6.

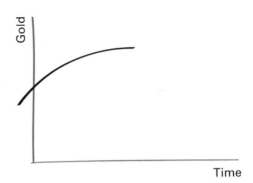

**Figure 4.6**
Gold inventory that changes at a decreasing rate

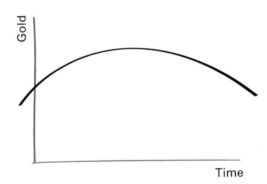

**Figure 4.7**
Gold inventory that changes at a decreasing rate

If the loop starts out with a gold velocity of +30 per trip, this tweak adds deceleration. Now velocity changes over time and for the worse. After some time, the loop turns from profitable to unprofitable, and if players keep iterating through it, they will start losing wealth as shown in figure 4.7.

This discourages grinding. Players will be much better off if they cut their losses before the expenses get too large and move on to another area in the game with different challenges and loops.

In practice, dynamic tuning can work very well if the player can control when to engage and disengage with the loop in question. It is more interesting for the player if they can make the decision of how long to try doing one thing and when to cut their losses and move on to something else that is perhaps more profitable or interesting.

## Feedback Loops

So far, we talked about loops whose behavior is stable and relatively static. Each time the player contributes some inputs and continues to crank through the loop, they will get some outputs, such as when hunting trolls, to get the loot that trolls carry. But many loops are not so static.

A *feedback system* is a different variant in which past behavior of the system affects its future behavior. Typically, this means there is some kind of *internal state* that drives the output of the system, and this output is then arranged to *feed back* into the system as one of the inputs and affects the state at a future time.

A common automotive example is cruise control, which maintains a desired velocity *set point*. As the vehicle travels, current velocity is checked against the set point and if it is too low, the system starts accelerating the vehicle. This in turn causes velocity to increase, eventually reaching the set point that will cause the system to turn acceleration off and let the vehicle coast. In this way, the system state and outputs form a *feedback loop*, reciprocally affecting each other over time.

Feedback loops are exceedingly common in natural and artificial systems, from animal populations to human control systems as we discuss below. They are very common in games as well, as they are often used to amplify or attenuate differences over time.

### Positive Feedback

A *positive feedback loop* is one where differences between the current state and the set point are processed and added back to the state causing the differences to increase over time. For a real-life example, consider *compound interest* in economics. Suppose we have a bank account with some money in it and each month an interest payment is paid out. That interest is then deposited back into the same account, so the second month's interest is based on both the principal and the interest accrued from the first month. Then the third interest payment is based on the principal amount and two months' worth of interest and so on.

Diagrammed, the feedback might look something like figure 4.8.

If we plotted the account over time assuming the interest rate is constant and positive, it might look something like the ever-increasing curve in figure 4.9.

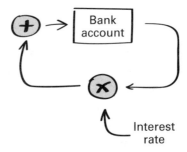

**Figure 4.8**
Diagram for bank account interest payments

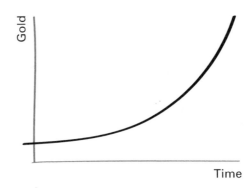

**Figure 4.9**
Bank account that increases at an ever-increasing rate

This a profitable loop for sure, but it also gets *more and more profitable* the more times you go through it! This is a *positive feedback* loop because feedback supports what the system was already doing. On each iteration, the difference from the set point of zero gets multiplied by the interest rate and added back to the account, which will *increase* the difference next time around.[8]

This kind of feedback produces powerful buildup and amplification of initial state. The multiplication step leads to runaway exponential growth.

Positive feedback loops are very common in games. *Monopoly* is every designer's favorite example of a long-term positive feedback loop. The

---

8. Sometimes these loops are also called *divergent* because each iteration causes the value to diverge further and further from the set point. Sellers (2017, 61) also uses the term *reinforcing loops*, as they reinforce and amplify initial advantages.

player with more money can buy or upgrade more properties, which means they collect more rent, which increases their chances of getting even more money. On the other hand, the player with less money has fewer chances to collect rent and fewer chances to acquire more land.

RTS and strategy games often use divergent feedback loops as well. In *StarCraft* players mine minerals that they can spend to build units and other things. But one of those units are harvesters that will let them mine even more minerals per unit of time. This positive feedback loop (get minerals, build harvesters, get even more minerals, build even more harvesters, etc.) is fortunately kept in check by having a hard cap on the amount of resources that could be harvested, as well as having other crucial systems that consume those minerals.

Similar effects are also present in single-player games. For example, farming-oriented games like *Stardew Valley* or *FarmVille* feature a very intuitive positive loop. The more plants are planted, the more bountiful the harvest, which means even more seeds or money for the next round of planting, and so on.

## Negative Feedback

A *negative feedback loop* is one that seeks to minimize differences between current and desired state. The previously mentioned cruise control is one typical example. Another stereotypical example is that of a thermostat hooked up to a room heating and cooling unit (Wiener 1961, 96).

Suppose we have a thermostat set to some desired temperature and it periodically monitors room temperature. If the room is too cold, current temperature is lower than set point, so a heater starts up to increase temperature and reduce the difference, as shown in figure 4.10.

Similarly, if the room is too warm, current temperature is higher than set point, so a cooling element is engaged to bring the temperature down and similarly reduce the difference.

Negative feedback loops are called that because feedback opposes what the system was already doing. The difference from the set point produces actions to reduce this difference in the future. In these kinds of systems, feedback pushes the system to converge towards the set point.[9]

---

9. For this reason, they are sometimes called *convergent loops*, or per Sellers (2017, 61), *balancing loops*.

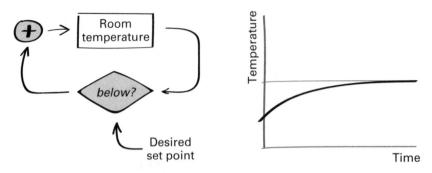

**Figure 4.10**
Diagram for a heating circuit and corresponding temperature chart

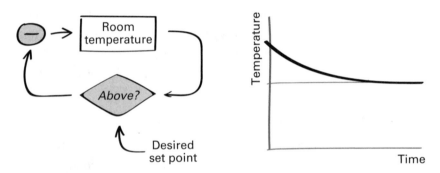

**Figure 4.11**
Diagram for a cooling circuit and corresponding temperature chart

Negative feedback is less common in games but still present in some cases. One example is dynamically changing the game depending on how well the player is doing to make an easy game harder and a difficult challenge easier.

Racing games sometimes employ *rubber-banding*—if the player is doing very poorly in the race, computer drivers will slow down to make sure not to get too far ahead, but if the player is leading the pack, drivers will pick up speed to make it harder for the player to win. In racing games where drivers get power-ups (which buff or nerf their abilities), the same effect can be achieved by modulating the quality of power-ups. For example, *Super Monkey Ball* makes it more likely for losing players to get speed-up buffs compared to players who are ahead of the pack (Salen and Zimmerman 2004, 221).

Similarly, some role-playing games might monitor when the player is entering a new area of the game and auto-tune enemy stats up or down based on the player's own level and stats. This is intended to make sure that the player gets challenged in ways that the designer anticipated even if the player went to the effort of training up their character to be at a higher level than expected or, on the flip side, if the player neglected to level up the character as much as was expected.

These can be considered as simple methods of dynamic difficulty adjustment. Additional methods are also possible, such as changing loot drop rates or quality, changing the distribution of enemies or materials in the level, and so on, depending on how far the player's state diverges from the expected state.

### Effects of Positive Feedback

Positive feedback loops have some nice effects on the player experience. It feels good to see your armies or bank accounts grow. It satisfies player motivations for power and control. It also reflects many of the natural and human-made systems that we are familiar with, such as a fast-growing population overtaking an ecosystem or the winner-takes-all tendencies of unregulated markets.[10]

However, positive feedback loops have the effect of amplifying early advantages. In single-player games, the effect might be benign. The player who invests in early growth will be rewarded by achieving higher wealth later. To prevent this from turning into a boring runaway feedback loop, designers typically add a variety of trade-offs to make the player think twice about whether to let the loop feed itself or spend the resources on something else.

To use an example from *StarCraft*, early in the game the player is faced with decisions about how to spend their minerals, which are a currency used to build various units and buildings. A variety of spending options is

---

10. There is an entire subgenre called "idle games," including titles like *Cookie Clicker* or *AdVenture Capitalist*, which focus almost entirely on ever-increasing positive feedback loops. In idle games, the player spends money or resources to build units that produce even more money or resources faster and faster, and it is surprisingly enjoyable to blow up production loops to absurdly large proportions (Pecorella 2016).

available, but one of the units is a harvester which digs up more minerals over time.

If the player spends their initial minerals to build one harvester (and nothing else), their mineral budget might look like the graph in figure 4.12 (for the sake of this example we assume this rate is constant over time).

The single harvester will provide minerals at velocity $x$ to fund future purchases. However, if the player decides to spend these resources on an additional second harvester, they will have to wait longer to have useful minerals, but at that point they will be producing them at $2x$ velocity. We can see the effect in figure 4.13.

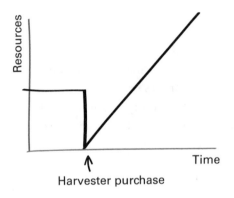

**Figure 4.12**
Illustration of mineral resources in *StarCraft* before and after a harvester purchase

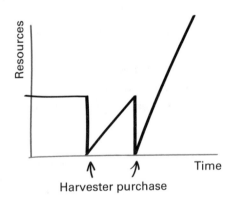

**Figure 4.13**
Illustration of mineral resources in *StarCraft* affected by the purchase of two harvesters over time

This is an interesting strategic decision point for the player, whether to "eat the seed corn" and reduce the later harvest or go hungry longer to produce a bountiful harvest later—and how to evaluate this vis-à-vis other needs that must be funded, such as building armed units to attack or defend oneself. Making decisions about which feedback loops to feed and which to pause leads to interesting strategic dilemmas.

However, in multiplayer games (or games with AI players), positive feedback might lead to an undesirable situation. If players engage in loops that feed back on themselves, the player who got an early advantage, even if small, may eventually outpace the other player. If the difference between players' resources grows too large to a point where the losing players cannot catch up and bridge this gap, it will have a destructive effect on the overall feel of fairness and competition.

For example, we consider the early stages of a war game where the player's army conquers lands, which lets them build and feed a larger army, which lets them conquer more lands, and so on. Let's say there are two players, and Player 1 got a bit of a head start in the beginning. Since army size and land conquest form a positive feedback loop, the players' overall resources (including army units) might look like in figure 4.14.

Both are growing in a divergent way, but since Player 1 had a better beginning the *gap* between them is increasing rapidly as well. At some point they may drift so far apart that Player 2 will never be able to catch up to Player 1, and if Player 2 realizes that their position is unwinnable, that will likely make the game much less enjoyable from that point on.

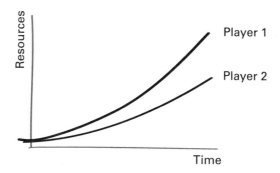

**Figure 4.14**
Illustration of player resource trajectories diverging over time as a result of slightly different initial conditions

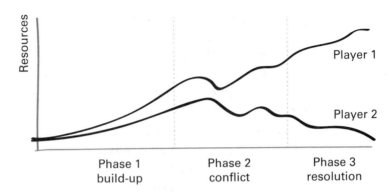

**Figure 4.15**
Initially divergent trajectories can affect the players in later stages of the game

An example of how it might play out is shown in figure 4.15.

If the difference between the players is too large, once Player 1 realizes their advantage, they will force Player 2 into a conflict (combat, arms race, etc.) where Player 2 will have a hard time keeping up. Then at some point it will become clear who the victor is going to be, and the game enters a *resolution phase* where players escalate conflict and spend down their resources to settle the winner. This resolution will be far less enjoyable for players who know they don't have a fighting chance.

*Monopoly* is especially famous for amplifying early wins and having a very long and tedious resolution phase as the winning player slowly erodes the bank accounts of the other players, forcing them into bankruptcy. That is a slow *war of attrition*, where two sides chip away at each other's resources, and the side with the most resources is most likely to win.

War of attrition is a common source of complaints among more advanced players. Since the outcome becomes obvious not too long into the game and the rest of it is a long resolution, an example graph for *Monopoly* might look like figure 4.16.

In comparison, games feel better if they have more interesting buildup and conflict phases, with more time spent in competition as players try to position themselves for victory, and a shorter resolution phase. RTS games like *StarCraft* often aim for a conflict phase where victory is uncertain, and a skilled player has many ways in which to turn a losing situation around, leading to a graph that perhaps looks like figure 4.17.

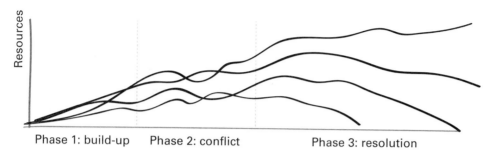

Phase 1: build-up    Phase 2: conflict         Phase 3: resolution

**Figure 4.16**
Example of a game with slowly diverging resource trajectories and a drawn-out resolution phase

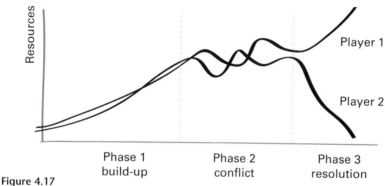

Player 1

Player 2

| Phase 1 | Phase 2 | Phase 3 |
| build-up | conflict | resolution |

**Figure 4.17**
Example of a game with close resource trajectories and a short resolution phase

### Effects of Negative Feedback

Negative or balancing feedback loops can be used to adjust the game to the player's abilities or perhaps to some desired type of play, but this too can have a negative impact.

In a single-player game, such as the role-playing game we described before, we could adjust enemies automatically to match the player's current level and character stats. This will provide a consistent challenge regardless of the player's prior successes or failures. But at the same time, it will make the player's past successes *less meaningful*. The reward for getting better should be that things get easier, and if getting better instead means the world just becomes more difficult, it makes the player wonder why they should try to get better in the first place.

In multiplayer games there is another effect. For example, in a racing game with rubber-banding, negative feedback is going to keep both players close together regardless of how well or how poorly they do. In effect, their early actions will matter much less than maneuvering into the front of the pack in the final lap. In this case, only the last moments of the game matter, and the game leading up to it will feel unrewarding if the player's early performance is inconsequential.

Games that rely heavily on randomization (like card games, children's board games, but also some computer games) often suffer from a similar effect as well, because if the random effect is too strong, it has a similar effect to rubber-banding in the sense that it can easily obliterate the player's entire performance so far and render their early effort useless.

Ultimately, games must combine both positive and negative feedback, rewarding players' performance in early game making it meaningful and useful but also preventing it from biasing the outcome too early. Unfortunately, this is easier said than done, and it routinely requires a lot of tweaks, tuning, and playtesting to get right.

### Emergence and Chaos

Individual systems are already complex, but an even more difficult analysis awaits us when we consider entire collections of systems. Like in the saying about "not seeing the forest for the trees," we might observe different behavior if we look at an entire collection of entities together compared to just a single entity at a time. In this section we look at two such phenomena in system analysis: emergent behavior and chaotic behavior.

### Emergent Behavior

If we zoom out and analyze a collection of entities as a single unit, we may observe behaviors which arise from, but are not predicted by, the behavior of the constituent elements. We call these *emergent behaviors*. Some natural examples include:

- Schools of fish and flocks of birds can be modeled as a single group that navigates through space and avoids obstacles even though it arises out of very simple flocking rules that each member follows, such as rules about maintaining momentum, avoiding flying into neighbors, and steering towards the center of the group (Reynolds n.d.).

- Ant hills and insect hives are highly organized structures formed by insects following simple, local rules, seemingly without needing to understand the overall structure.

- At the extreme end of the spectrum, eukaryotes such as ourselves are examples of organized entities that emerge out of the countless individual cells following rules and organizing themselves into tissues, organs, and systems that have specific properties.

A behavior is considered emergent if it is not easily predicted from the behaviors of constituent elements and yet exhibits properties that are stable over time.[11] Because emergent behaviors are not easily predicted, they can be hard to design intentionally. Instead, it is easier to discover them by experimenting with different system implementations.

Emergent behavior can be controversial. Given the designer's goal of creating a specific experience for the player, using emergent behaviors requires a lot of work to try out different experiments, observe, tune, and make sure the system behaviors are desirable. This makes them less suitable for the kinds of games which require tight control over the quality and predictability of the player's experience, such as linear story-based action games.

And yet, some games are keen to employ emergent behaviors as part of the desirable experience in spite of their unpredictability—for example, games that center on procedural generation and simulation as well as massively multiplayer games.

In simulation games, part of the fun of the experience is being faced with a collection of complex systems with unpredictable emergent characteristics and trying to control and manage them, or perhaps just letting them run and observing what they do. One anecdote from the game *Dwarf Fortress* illustrates this point. In the game, players build and manage underground dwarf settlements. The game is full of systems with emergent interactions, and one example of such interaction became well known. At some point players discovered that cats in the fortress sometimes got drunk, which was not expected or coded intentionally, so how did it happen? It turned out to be a collection of systems working together in unexpected ways. At one

---

11. Sellers (2017, 78) calls these behaviors *metastable*, since they are markedly different from behaviors of the constituent elements and yet remain stable even as the individual constituent behaviors changes dynamically. For example, individual birds fly along different trajectories, and yet the entire flock seems to behave as one.

point, taverns were added to the game and dwarves who bought beer would clumsily spill it on the floor. Another system implemented liquid tracking via footprints, and the cat behavior system guided cat hygiene and self-cleaning, and yet another system guided ingestion of substances and their effects. All these ended up working together in unexpected ways. Dwarves spilled beer, cats walked through it, got it on their paws, and when they cleaned themselves they ingested the beer and got drunk (Fenlon 2016).

Multiplayer games often exhibit emergent behavior as well because human players bring their social behaviors, structures, and expectations into the game, such as tendencies to organize, cooperate, compete, and form larger social structures to accomplish larger goals. Large scale MMOs often display and explicitly support these kinds of social behaviors. MMO games such as *EVE Online* host very large social structures where individuals work together as corporations to compete with other corporations, in an ecosystem that supports emergent groups of all sizes from very large teams to individual lone wolves (see Lehdonvirta and Castranova (2014) for great examples). The emergent properties of human social structures are even harder to reason about, but fortunately we have a lot of intuitions about how we behave and a lifetime of experience compared to our experience with analyzing other systems.

Emergent behavior arises out of systems or their elements working together and often surprises us in unexpected ways. This can be a great asset or an enormous liability, depending on the designer's intentions, desire for control, and intended player experience. It creates gameplay that the player did not expect from interacting with the individual elements. However, making sure the emergent behavior remains within desirable parameters is a difficult task.

### Chaotic Systems

Games will often employ multiple systems with simultaneous feedback loops that feed into each other. This kind of a setup often turns *chaotic*, which is to say it is a system where slight changes to the inputs can produce drastically different behavior over time so it becomes difficult to predict analytically how it will behave at a future point. This term derives from *chaos theory*, the study of dynamical systems that exhibit these kinds of properties.

Animal populations in an ecosystem are popular examples of chaotic feedback loops which may or may not exhibit metastable properties. For example, each species of animals in a forest has its own population dynamics. Some individuals will give birth and some will die, and the population will grow as long as birth rate exceeds death rate and the resources support it (e.g., food and space). But what if the food of one population is another population, such as foxes hunting rabbits? This is the case with ecological "predator and prey" models. These two populations depend on each other in different ways. Predator population grows when there is prey to capture, and prey population grows when there are fewer predators.

The result are two feedback loops that modulate each other. Growing fox population will decimate rabbits, but that will cause foxes to run out of prey and starve, which in turn might allow the rabbit population to rebound, so the effect might look something like figure 4.18.

Simple chaotic systems may sometimes be modeled analytically using differential equations (such as the Lotka–Volterra model for predator and prey interactions), but more complex ecologies typically defy analytic solution and must be simulated. The actual ecosystem of an area, such as a local forest or a river basin, is a collection of a large number of feedback loops that, just by its sheer scale, typically exhibits chaotic properties but resists analysis.

Human systems can also be chaotic. Economies, for example, are very complex, human-made feedback systems—large networks of multiple producers and consumers all collaborating and competing at the same time. On the micro level, the economic study of *supply chains* focuses on the real-world resource production and consumption feedback loops, but it is difficult to scale them to macro-level analysis. They also often exhibit chaotic

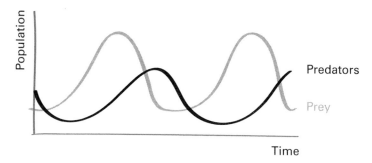

**Figure 4.18**

Example population and prey population size over time, patterned after Sellers (2017, 64)

properties. A small change in initial conditions can be amplified over time to lead to a very different situation later, which makes their behavior difficult to predict.

The following example of games imitating life shows systems exhibiting properties that are both emergent and chaotic, and illustrates some of the difficulties with designing them. The early MMO game *Ultima Online* was one of the few online games to try to model its ecosystem somewhat realistically, at least initially. New players had to hunt rabbits and small prey to get meat and pelts, which they would sell for money to buy a sword and some armor to finally venture out in search of adventure. But hunting animals would decrease their population in the ecosystem, which then affected how quickly the population bounced back to previous levels, as well as affecting other species in the ecosystem that needed them.

Once the game went into testing with more players, these loops turned disastrous. New players could initially only hunt small prey, so they emptied the forests of small animals to raise enough money. With the population not replacing itself fast enough, the next cohort of players who joined after them found themselves with no way to make money or do anything meaningful in the game, which made the game *really not fun*.

In the end, the dynamic ecosystem simulation had to be scrapped and replaced with nonlooping chains of stable sources and sinks. Animals would just spawn at a desired rate to maintain a population, and local merchants bought them at fixed prices so that new players would always have a source of easy money. Although it was not realistic, at least it was predictable and tunable and it made the game reasonable for new players (Ward 2003) (Garriott 2017).

## Systems Design

Now that we have seen a variety of systems in general and in detail, how do we get started on them?

The basic approach is iterative. We need to alternate coming up with building blocks, putting them together, and seeing how they work. As we discussed back in chapter 1, there are two basic directions to start from:

1. *Bottom up*, creating and testing a single system, then adding on another one and testing how they work together, and so on. In this way systems accrue and accumulate over time.

2. *Top down*, imagining what gameplay would be like, describing it, and then figuring out what systems are needed to make this gameplay happen and how they interact with each other.

Both approaches are used in game development. The bottom-up approach is more exploratory and lets the designer experiment and see where the exploration takes them. The top down approach is more common when there is a specific end goal or experience that we want to evoke and we need to figure out how exactly to do it. Both approaches can also be used together, in which case we would use top down analysis to figure out some necessary systems but also experiment and explore to build on that base in unexpected directions.

## From User Stories to Systems

The top down approach can seem complex. We might have big ideas for gameplay but also have difficulty translating them into specific systems. To make this process easier, we can employ an iterative technique to help us list out a variety of systems that will be needed.

We start with a "user story," a narrative description of a bit of gameplay, and then we analyze what kinds of systems or mechanics are entailed by that user story. Then we analyze what kinds of systems or mechanics are in turn entailed by those, and so on, iteratively filling in our design with each pass.

For example, let's say we want to make a tower defense game where lines of creeps follow a specific path to reach the player's base and the player sets up a defense perimeter to shoot them down before they get there.

First, we write out a narrative about the desired experience:

Creeps are spawned in waves and follow a specific path to reach a player's home base. The player can build towers to shoot them down before they get there. The game is over when any creep reaches the home base.

(There is much more that we could describe but we will stop here to keep this example simple.)

Second, we go through this simple narrative sentence by sentence, word by word, and mark it up. What kinds of systems are implied by the narrative? What do we need to make this happen?

For example, table 4.1 lists a number of elements mentioned in the narrative:

**Table 4.1**
Narrative marked up with elements to be defined and implemented

| Narrative | Terms to define |
|---|---|
| Creeps are spawned in waves and follow a specific path to reach a player's home base. The player can build towers to shoot them down before they get there. The game is over when any creep reaches the home base. | Creeps |
| | Spawning |
| | Following a path |
| | Towers |
| | Building |
| | Shooting |
| | Game over |

- We need some kinds of enemies, or "creeps," to try to capture the player's home.
- We need a system to spawn those enemies in waves.
- We need pathfinding or some predetermined paths and handmade levels.
- We need buildings (towers) to shoot down the creeps.
- We need the ability to build and place those towers.
- We need a combat system to determine how shooting will work.
- We need victory conditions and loss conditions.

Next, we go through this list and ask ourselves, for each item, how will it work?

*We need some kinds of enemies or "creeps" to try to capture the player's home. What does this mean?*
Creeps should be simple and dumb entities that march towards the end goal. They will get shot at by the player, so they need some defensive abilities. Let's say a few can counterattack. They need some attack abilities as well. There should also be multiple types of creeps to provide variety.

*We need a system to create those enemies in waves. What does this mean?*
We want fewer and easier creeps initially, and then have the game ramp them up to increase difficulty. We need a spawner to keep track of time in each level and create the right type and number of creeps. The designer needs to be able to specify different waves per level.

*Creeps need to be able to find their way towards the home base. What does this mean?*

Let's say levels are freeform so the player can place buildings anywhere. We need a pathfinding system for creeps to find their way.

*We need towers to shoot down the creeps. What does this mean?*

These will be buildings that can be placed but not moved. Placement matters. And just like creeps, towers need to have defensive and offensive abilities, but the attack ability needs to be limited to some range to make placement interesting. To add variety, we want to have different towers with stat trade-offs: more defense or more offense, better or worse firing range or speed, and so on. The player should be able to upgrade a tower to buff its stats.

*We need the ability to build towers. What does this mean?*

There should be different costs for placing or upgrading towers with different stats. If there is a cost, there needs to be a currency and a way to earn it. Let's say the player earns currency by clearing out a wave of creeps. Creeps should be worth different amounts of currency based on type and stats.

*We need a combat system to determine how shooting will work. What does this mean?*

We're going to use attack and defense points and health bars as seen in RPGs. The difference between those determines how much health is lost during an attack. Towers (and creeps that attack) also need a firing rate, which will be different for different unit types.

*We need victory conditions and loss conditions. What does this mean?*

The game ends when a creep survives and reaches the player's base. We decide the game cannot be "won"; it's just an endless sequence of levels. We can make the levels increase in difficulty. To mark progression, we also add a score, which increases more quickly on harder levels. We also add a high score table and leaderboards for competitive players.

As you can see, a simple three-sentence description of gameplay can easily imply a lot of mechanics and systems—combat, construction, pathfinding, progression, economy, and so on. And even within those, we have already started discussing some very specific mechanics—attack and defense points, buffs and upgrades to improve those points, weapons, area of effect ranges, and currencies and how they can be earned and spent.

In this top-down part of the design process, we generate narrative descriptions like these for different parts of gameplay and then try to figure out what systems and mechanics would make that kind of gameplay happen. Then once we have some ideas about systems and mechanics, we can switch over to a bottom-up design mode, figure out in which order to build them, and then try to stand up a simple prototype to test our design ideas.

But we do not have to wait until the prototyping phase to start experimenting with our design. Even before the prototyping stage, we can consider additional ideas purely "on paper" by imagining in detail what their consequences would be. For example:

*What would happen if we added a spell and magic system?*
Maybe spells could support combat and provide new kinds of weapons and upgrades, but instead of paying with a currency, we acquire them via casting spells.

*But how do we get spells?*
Maybe the player needs to collect scrolls to unlock spells and accumulate mana points to actually "fuel" them.

*But how do we get mana?*
Maybe specific kinds of creeps drop mana as they walk and scrolls are something you can research by spending currency on building a research tower? Does this mean we need to add research towers? How do they work?
… And so on.

By combining top-down analysis based on a desired narrative, as well as experimenting with new directions and evaluating where they lead, the designer can perform a kind of guided exploration of the system design space. This kind of exploration gets easier as we become familiar with numerous examples of systems, in other games as well as other areas of life, to be able to draw on existing models and bring them to our own game.

## System Tuning

In the previous section we imagined the general structure of systems and mechanics in a tower defense game. Once we implement this structure, we will also need to figure out how *exactly* the pieces of this structure will interact. How much will a tower cost and what currency will be used? How many attack and defense points will each creep have? How much currency do we get for killing a creep?

This process of finding those exact numeric values and making those low-level decisions is called *tuning* the game. Tuning is often an iterative process, largely guided by experience and playtesting, and finding the correct balance for all these moving parts takes work. If the game is tuned too *tight*, such as when it is quite difficult for the player to progress and succeed, the game will be more challenging but also more frustrating for players who are not sufficiently experienced. Likewise, if a game is tuned too *loose*, when the rewards are plentiful and challenges are easy, this will make life easier for a new player but will frustrate and bore an experienced player.

However, there might not even be a "middle ground" for tuning that satisfies all player types, which is why so many games attempt to add multiple difficulty levels as a stop-gap solution. Worse yet, since different parts of the game get tuned separately, we could arrive at a game that feels inconsistent. For example, if combat is tuned too easy so creeps die quickly and the economy is tuned too hard so we cannot afford new towers easily, this will be bound to frustrate players across all skill levels.

### Approaches

There are four basic approaches to system tuning: manual tuning, building external models of the game, using the game itself to do simulated runs, and collecting performance stats from human players and analyzing them in aggregate.

*Manual tuning* is the obvious case. We have some ideas about what to improve, so we go into the game, change some content (tuning variables, level layout, etc.), and play it to see how it works. Based on the playtest, we form a hypothesis about what to change next and repeat. Sometimes those changes will be improvements but at other times they will cause problems and need to be undone. But in this way, we improve the game iteratively by repeating the tune-and-test steps until we reach a satisfactory state. This approach is slow, but thorough—because the designer keeps playing the game, they can observe how the tuning changes not only affect the system in question, but also what knock-on effects they have on other systems. Unfortunately, the amount of gameplay required for thorough testing is prohibitively large (because games have enormous state spaces), so designers rely on compartmentalization (playtesting specific parts of the game in separation) and experience to figure out how the game will play based on just limited testing.

To remove the need for gameplay testing, designers sometimes build *models* of the game systems in software such as Microsoft Excel. This is particularly useful for numbers-heavy systems such as economy or combat. In this case, the designer creates a simplified model of just the systems in question and simulates how the model would evolve given some player inputs. This is much faster than manual tuning but has a significant drawback: because the spreadsheet is just a model of some game systems it will inevitably be simpler and different from what is in the game itself. This means the model is limited in scope and can lead to erroneous conclusions depending on the how well the model corresponds to the game.

This discrepancy between model and base game can be fixed in a different way—we can use the game itself by feeding it artificially prepared player inputs and seeing how it plays out. This *simulation* would be a kind of automated testing and it could be much faster than manual testing (maybe the system could play the game at much higher speed or we could parallelize testing across a farm of computers). This approach is difficult and expensive, however. The game must be instrumented for this kind of forward simulation and we must find a way to produce a variety of fake player inputs for testing, which is actually quite hard for games of nontrivial complexity. One feasible work-around to this limitation is to limit simulation testing to just a single system (such as economy or combat), which means we only need to produce player inputs for a specific subset of relevant actions (such as buying and selling and earning currency). This is easier than trying to have the computer play the full game, but it shares some of the drawbacks with spreadsheet modeling (Tozour 2013).

The last approach is to release the game to players (maybe a limited beta test group or maybe to all players), collect data on what they actually do, and tune the game accordingly. This approach based on *analytics* has several benefits. The results are based on actual player behavior rather than assumptions or models about how they might play the game, and players in large numbers tend to be very good at finding edge cases and dominant strategies. However, this is not a sufficient replacement for other forms of tuning. Some other tuning must happen first because if we ship a poorly tuned game to testers, they will have a difficult time with it and we will not get good quality feedback. However, analytics are great for fine-tuning systems that are already in a roughly good shape or for finding dominant or degenerate strategies not foreseen by the designer. Analytics are also often used for iterative feature roll-out and tuning, that is, releasing a new feature of the game to a small number of players first to confirm that it behaves as expected (and to retune it quickly if it does not) before releasing it to all players.

### The Role of Tuning in the Production Process

Regardless of the approach, tuning usually happens many times during a game's lifetime—during the *development* of individual systems, then during *integration* of multiple systems together, as well as during a *polish* phase when the entire game comes together.

When developing a single system, it is usually a good idea to give it a rough tuning pass right during development—for example, making sure that character movement feels right in a platformer before moving on to level design. This does not have to be perfect, but once we integrate multiple systems together, tuning deficiencies in one system will affect the player's experience of the whole thing, so it is best to get ahead of that early on.

Once several systems are integrated, another tuning pass will be needed to iron out interactions between them. For example, in action games, it is common to revise the "3 Cs" (character, camera, and controls) together as early as possible because they all affect each other and they affect the player's experience with everything else.

Once the game comes together in an alpha state where all the systems are roughly in place, more holistic tuning can happen that considers the total experience and the player's interactions with all systems and content. At this stage, the tuning changes usually will have smaller scope, but standing up the entire game will often expose a very large number of deficiencies and opportunities for improvement.

In this sense, the tuning process is akin to a visual artist's process—we start with a rough sketch of the whole piece and then iteratively fill in the details.

### Summary

In this chapter we looked at game systems, which are built from simpler individual mechanics. The key takeaways are:

- *Systems* are collections of mechanics set up to work together in specific ways. Economy, inventory, combat, and other example systems are discussed in the context of the game *Diablo*.

  Systems are a useful design abstraction, letting us analyze games as collections of different groups of mechanics. However, systems should not be treated as fully separate; they should interlock and affect each other in interesting ways, for example, by using the same shared mechanics but for different purposes.

- It can be useful to look at systems as *chains* or *loops* of smaller interactions that produce some resources or convert them into others. For an example from the *Diablo* game series, mechanics around fighting, collecting loot, selling this loot for gold, and restocking and healing, come together to form a resource loop that links several systems (such as economy, inventory, and combat).

- *Conversion loops* can be analyzed in terms of their production rates and how they change over time as the player participates in them. Analysis can help us tune them to prevent exploits, such as players grinding through them to amass an excessive amount of resources.

- *Feedback loops* can happen when a system has an internal state that affects the output of the system, but this output feeds back to change the internal state, creating a scenario where the output and internal state reciprocally affect each other over time. *Positive feedback loops*, which amplify initial changes, and *negative feedback loops*, which counteract changes, are the two typical cases. Feedback loops are very common in games, but runaway feedback can lead to undesirable long-term behaviors, such as amplifying early advantages and making the game impossible to lose or impossible to win. Balancing these effects is central to systems design.

- Systems can also be *emergent* and *chaotic*. These are also common in the real world and familiar to players, but getting them to behave correctly and to be enjoyable for the player is a formidable challenge.

- How do we know what systems will be needed for some game we have in mind? We can start by creating user stories describing gameplay narratively and then trying to tease out what kind of specific systems and mechanics are required to implement this narrative.

- Finally, as we implement systems, we also need to remember to *tune* them as we go. For example, figure out the right specific item prices in the economy system, the right weapon stats in combat, and so on. The success of a system or a set of interacting systems is very sensitive to finding good tuning values, whether through experience or experimentation.

Having focused on mechanics and systems as standalone tools, we are now ready to switch to the next topic in our sequence. In the next chapter we talk about gameplay and about how interacting with mechanics and systems develops over time into the subjective experience of playing the game.

## Further Reading

The analysis of mechanics and systems and their interplay are the focus of *Advanced Game Design* (Sellers 2017) which is highly recommended for interested readers. For readers interested in more formal modeling of systems, *Game Mechanics: Advanced Game Design* (Adams and Dormans 2012) presents a very detailed modeling technique and suggests running those models in simulation to see how they behave at runtime before committing them to in-game implementation. This kind of formal models are also known as *game grammars*. Perhaps the earliest documented examples of this approach are in Koster's "A Grammar of Gameplay" (2005).

Outside of games, systems have been studied in many contexts, and economics and business management might be the most intuitively familiar. Economics textbooks such as *The Economy* (CORE Team 2017) can be great introductions to contemporary thinking about large scale and complicated systems such as the world economy. Classics of dynamic systems study such as *Industrial Dynamics* (Forrester 1961) and *Cybernetics* (Wiener 1961) may also be of historical interest.

## Individual Exercises

### 4.1. Game Systems
Both mechanics and systems are building blocks of game design, but they differ in scale and composition. How do you differentiate between mechanics and systems? Give an example of a game system and the mechanics that make it up.

### 4.2. System Layering
Pick a computer game you know very well.

a.  Try to write down as many of the systems in the game as you can think of with short descriptions of what they do (only a sentence or two each).

   b. Now pick some of those systems that share one or more common mechanics. Describe how they interact and the mechanics they share.

### 4.3. Chains and Loops

Pick a game you know well. Find a resource loop in that game (there may be multiple, in which case pick just one) and describe it in detail. Do you see profitable or unprofitable loops? Is there a profitable loop that could lead to runaway resource creation? Why or why not?

### 4.4. Grinding

The term "grinding" often refers to going through resource loops just to gain resources or to improve stats, but where the actual activity is not enjoyable or interesting.

   a. Can you think of a game in which you were grinding for something and not having fun? Describe that resource chain.

   b. Describe your own motivation for going through it. Why did you keep grinding through that loop?

   c. Now consider if that grind was completely removed. Would that improve the game? How do you think that would impact your experience?

### 4.5. Positive Feedback Loops

Pick a video or board game you know well that exhibits a strong positive feedback loop.

   a. Describe how the feedback loop amplifies the production of some resources based on its previous output.

   b. Now imagine that you can change this game so that the feedback loop is not so strongly self-reinforcing. Would it be desirable or even possible? How would it affect gameplay?

### 4.6. Feedback Loops

Pick a game where you play against other players or AI and describe the positive and/or negative loops present in the game. How do the loops present in the game affect the conflict and resolution phases?

## Group Exercises

### G4.1. Design Challenge: Speeding Up *Monopoly*

In this exercise, your goal is to speed up the gameplay of *Monopoly* by analyzing possible changes, implementing them, and then playtesting your new variant. (This exercise assumes you have access to this particular board game. The instructor may suggest substituting a different game in its place.)

   a. Play the board game *Monopoly* or one of its variants to remind yourself of gameplay. Then, consider how you could end the game faster by changing some of the mechanics and systems in the game. You are free to make any changes you would like. Some examples to consider: you can strengthen the "rich get richer" feedback loop (e.g., making rents higher or making them increase faster), you can remove the negative feedback elements that help players who are falling behind (e.g., removing the money reward when you pass "go," removing random chance cards, removing the ability to mortgage properties), and so on.

b.  Write down your changes to the rules and discuss how you think this will affect the speed of the game.

c.  Play the game again observing your feeling of how quickly players gain or lose money and win or lose the game compared to the original.

To complete the exercise, describe the following:

d.  In detail, describe the new changes, including the actions, pieces, and rules that are affected.

e.  Explain why you picked those particular changes and how you *expected* them to affect gameplay.

f.  Discuss how they *actually* affected gameplay as you observed during the playtest.

g.  Explain how you think they accomplished this—what it is about them that brought about these changes? Did the game feel faster or not and what accounted for this difference?

# 5   Gameplay

In the previous chapters we covered mechanics, the building blocks of gameplay, and assembling them into systems so that together they form chains, loops, and interlocked mechanisms. In this section we look at how these elements together produce gameplay.

*Gameplay* is what happens when we participate in an ongoing interaction with the game's mechanics and systems and potentially other players in multiplayer games. Gameplay is the *dynamic activity* that emerges out of player's interaction with mechanical elements, and participating in this interaction creates a certain experience for the player.

In this chapter we look at how we can systematically think about and analyze this gameplay. In the previous chapter we discussed feedback loops and systems. Now we will turn our attention to a different kind of a loop, in which the players and the game itself interact in the form of cyclical, repeating activities.

In the first part of the chapter we learn how to analyze games in terms of cyclical gameplay loops with various frequencies and how those loops interact with systems. Then in the second part of the chapter we look at player motivations for taking part in these loops and how we can support player motivation through gameplay design.

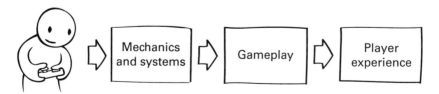

**Figure 5.1**
Recap of the basic model

### Motivating Example: *The Sims*

Let's say we are playing a session of *The Sims 4*. This is a game in which we control the lives of artificial people set in a simulated replica of a small town. We have complete control over our simulated people, but we need to keep them happy and fulfill their various needs, which are usually numerous and at odds with each other.

We are playing Alice and Bob's house, and Bob came back from work to see that Alice is throwing a party. Bob is exhausted and his energy is close to crashing. But at the same time, he feels unhappy because his social score is low and meeting someone new would really cheer him up.

We need to decide what he should do. Meeting someone new would be good, but he is also very tired. On one hand, he risks passing out from tiredness and oversleeping for work the next day. On the other hand, meeting new people will make him very happy and therefore more positive and efficient, a sure way to get that promotion that he has been working on. His life ambition is to become a CEO one day and a promotion would get him much closer. So, we make a decision—Bob will have to buck up, go out there, and socialize. This is for his own good. Sleep can wait for another time.

**Figure 5.2**
Screenshot from *The Sims 4*

Just that one decision point asked us to consider our choices and goals on several levels.

* *Short-term:* the need to maintain our sim's immediate well-being and urgent needs
* *Medium-term:* the need to make sure today and tomorrow are taken care of
* *Long-term:* the need to work towards the larger goals of becoming a CEO

As we play, we must consider goals and activities on different time scales at the same time. This is not accidental. Games deliberately present challenges on multiple levels simultaneously, and the various levels support each other. Without short-term challenges, there would be nothing interesting to do right here and now, and without long-term goals, there would be no reason to keep playing over a longer period.

Working towards goals on different time scales typically means engaging with *different systems* in the game. In *The Sims*, short-term planning is based on the "wants and needs" system, which gives sims different needs that need to be managed. For example, a hungry sim will need to find food very quickly otherwise bad things will happen. Medium-term planning is based on the "jobs" system and the game economy, in which sims can find jobs with different requirements, salaries, and work hours so that they can make the money to afford the things they need to succeed in the long term. Long-term planning is based on the "life goals" system in which a sim's long-term goal might be to become a CEO or a famous musician. Setting them up for success requires planning in advance and often spending money and time on things that have very delayed payoffs, such as taking evening classes or investing time in skill practice.

## Gameplay Loops

We have seen some activities in which the player engages repeatedly. We will call these *gameplay loops* since they are cyclical activities—the player keeps making decisions, acting on them, and then coming back to the same decision points.

In our *Sims* example, our smallest gameplay loop was *action selection*. We pick the next action to take (go to sleep, go socialize, go make dinner), wait for it to happen, see the effects (more energy, happier sim), and repeat. This happens very frequently, on the order of several times a minute.

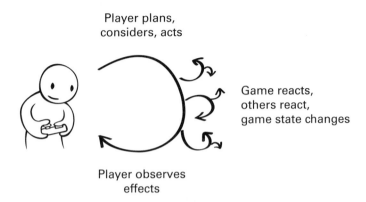

Player plans,
considers, acts

Game reacts,
others react,
game state changes

Player observes
effects

**Figure 5.3**
Player actions produce reactions from game systems and from other players to which
the player must react, forming a continuous loop

Then there are larger gameplay loops present as well at the same time.
For example, every morning in the game, we need to make sure the sim is
well rested, going to work, and making money. This requires different kinds
of decisions maybe every few minutes of real time. Finally, on a multiday
basis, we need to make sure they are improving their skills and advancing their career. These kinds of larger decisions do not come as frequently,
maybe every ten or twenty minutes, but they also require attention.

**Loop Frequencies**
Gameplay loops have different *frequencies*. A fast loop turns over every few
seconds or minutes of game time, and a very slow loop (like working towards
a career goal) only requires infrequent decisions.

For other examples of gameplay loops, we can look briefly at a dungeon
crawler game like *Diablo*, described in the previous chapter.

- Every few seconds (also known as the *micro* level): move, attack, defend,
  cast spell, equip, take, drop
- Every minute or two: find enemies, battle enemies, collect loot, locate
  treasure
- Every five to ten minutes: venture out from camp, clear out a section,
  return and sell loot, heal
- Every fifteen to thirty minutes: clear out the entire area, change up crew,
  level up characters

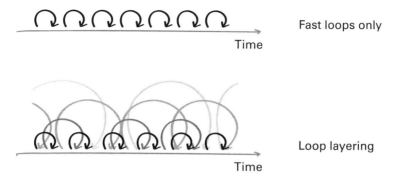

**Figure 5.4**
Comparison of a sequence of fast loops only with a combination of layered loops of varying frequencies

- Every few hours: explore an entire region of the game world, advance the story

Loops with different frequencies are active *at the same time*. The player's attention will be most focused on actions on the micro level, focusing on the immediate situation. But these actions also have macro consequences, so players must keep all levels in mind as they play so they can slowly advance long-term loops while they interact with the shorter ones.

As designers, we must plan for all loops to be active and design the game with multiple frequencies of decision making in mind.

### Onion Diagrams

A popular way to diagram gameplay loops visually is using *onion diagrams*. Figure 5.5 shows an example onion diagram from a (simplified) description of *Monopoly*, which will also illustrate the reason for this name.

The fastest, smallest loop starts out in the center, then ones with longer and longer periods get displayed around it. We can imagine that as the player iterates through the smallest loop over and over, they will also progress through the outer layers as well but less quickly and only partially.

A few more examples from *Diablo* and *The Sims*, also simplified, are shown in figure 5.6.

Onion diagrams are mainly a communication tool. They make it very easy to document and communicate to others what kinds of gameplay loops exist in the design.

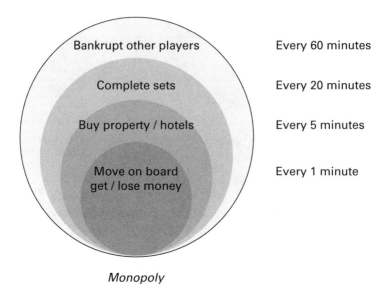

**Figure 5.5**
Simplified onion diagram for *Monopoly*

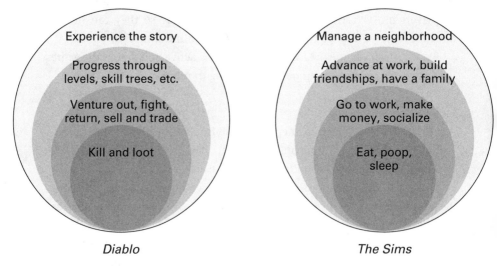

**Figure 5.6**
Simplified onion diagrams for *Diablo* and *The Sims* games

Since a game will also want to have a good distribution of loops at various frequencies, an onion diagram will easily show if we have a gap someplace that we need to fill in with interesting activity.

## The Core Loop

Designing interlocked activities is complicated, so it can be beneficial to start by focusing on the *core loop* first and evolve the design from there. This is the "minimum viable" level of activity, the smallest kind of a loop that's going to be *meaningful* and *enjoyable* to the player and give them a reason to keep playing.

In some game types, the smallest loop or *micro loop* is also the core loop because micro-level activities already provide challenge that keeps the player interested. This is more common in action games, for example in a driving game just mastering physical movement and keeping the car on the road while passing the others to get into the lead might be challenging enough.

In other games, however, the core loop will need to be slightly more complex than just micro actions. This is particularly the case in more systems-heavy games in which micro actions are not sufficiently challenging and not enough to motivate the player to keep playing. In a game like *The Sims*, just keeping track of physical needs might not be challenging, and the core loop is higher up on the level of "go to work, make money, come back, buy some stuff for the house, repeat." In *Diablo*, it might be "go out and fight, collect loot, come back to camp, sell it, buy or upgrade gear, repeat."

The core loop requires a lot of attention because the player will be interacting with it *all the time*, so we need to make sure they enjoy it even as their attention shifts towards harder problems with a longer time horizon. This problem is amplified by players' varying skill levels and advanced players may not be as drawn by the core loop as novice players.

## Layering

The core loop is also a convenient starting point for building a larger game on top of it—for example, using the following steps:

1. Start with a micro loop that involves doing small things in the game. This typically will not be very interesting but will be interactive and lets the designer test out the basics.

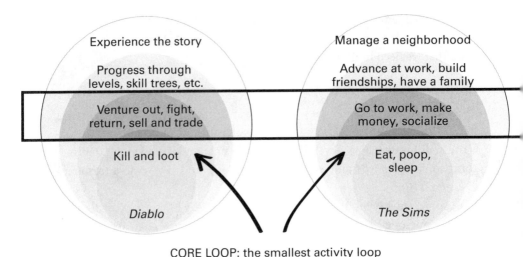

CORE LOOP: the smallest activity loop
that the player will find interesting

**Figure 5.7**
Onion diagrams from figure 5.6 with the core loops highlighted

2. Explore and grow the micro loop to find the core loop. This is the point where the game starts being enjoyable to play over the short term on the level of minutes. Once identified, we spend some time iterating on the core loop to improve it and to explore ideas about how to extend it.

3. At this point, we can start layering on longer term loops. If we have not designed those yet, exploring the core loop should give us ideas about larger loops that make the player interested over a longer time. These larger loops should *support* smaller ones by interacting with them or their outputs.

In *The Sims*, for example, we described an engaging core loop of making and spending money and managing the sim's physical needs. But this loop by itself has relatively short-term appeal. Adding larger loops that challenge it, such as adding family members or having a career to advance in, will change up the parameters of how to play the core loop and keep it fresh and interesting in addition to adding long-term challenges.

Advancing in one loop does not have to advance other loops, and it might be more interesting if the various loops are slightly at odds. Some game types seem to delight in making the layers work against each other, which gives the player a considerable challenge. *Factorio*, for example, is a resource production and logistics game in which the player manages complex production chains and spatial layout of the "factory" is of utmost importance. However, the player's objectives in early game will push them towards layouts that become a serious problem later in the game and need to be worked around or undone and rebuilt. Figuring out how to balance short term early game goals with future long-term objectives becomes a major source of fun and often frustration.

## Loops and Systems

Gameplay loops come from engaging with mechanics and systems as well as other players. Different frequencies are often supported by different game systems that work together as already highlighted at the beginning of this section in *The Sims* example.

For another example, we come back to dungeon crawlers. We have already mentioned the loop of leaving camp, clearing out an area, and coming back with loot. Then each time we come back to base camp, we have a variety of goals we can try to advance: economic development (selling and trading loot), developing our characters (leveling them up or training), crafting (such as upgrading weapons), and so on. These in turn serve to advance different longer-term goals as well: amassing wealth, character and story advancement, or ensuring that we have much better weapons for later battles.

Just like we listed out activities for each loop, we can turn it around and match loops to systems and mechanics, for example as listed in table 5.1 below.

**Table 5.1**
Examples of game loops and systems that support them

| Frequency | Gameplay loops | Example of related systems |
| --- | --- | --- |
| **every minute or two** | find enemies, battle enemies, collect loot, locate treasure | exploration, combat, items, stats, currencies, inventory |
| **every five to ten minutes** | venture out from camp, clear out a section, return and sell loot, heal | exploration, items, inventory, economy, crafting, upgrades, stats, skills |
| **every fifteen to thirty minutes** | clear out the entire area, change up crew, level up characters | inventory, crafting, character specialization, collectibles |
| **every few hours** | explore an entire region of the game world, advance the story | character specialization, crew management, campaign/story arc |

We can see that *various loops and frequencies often involve specific systems* (as opposed to having systems that work across *all* frequencies). This is because different systems have different behaviors and are tuned in different ways. It is difficult to devise a single system that would present the player with interesting challenges at all the various frequencies from micro- to long-term.

However, loops often share systems with their "neighbors." For example, inventory and stats participate in several loops across different frequencies. This is desirable because it means that a single action that advances one loop can also affect (advance or revert) progress in other loops, which makes those actions more strategically interesting.

Finally, some of these loops focus on more than interaction; they also pull in narrative and storytelling elements. In a story-driven RPG like *Dragon Age: Origins*, some of the shorter loops tend to focus on combat, leveling up, and other such systems. However, the long-term player motivation comes from a gripping narrative that drives the player to want to learn what will happen next and want to take actions that will affect the unfolding story. We will come back to the analysis of these kinds of narrative elements later on, in chapter 6, "Macrostructure."

## Player Motivation

We have looked at how mechanics and systems produce gameplay by giving the player a variety of activities and challenges that arise out of interaction with them. The player interacts with them repeatedly, forming loops of repeated activity with different frequencies. By layering challenges with different time horizons together we give the player a stream of gameplay which challenges them in the short as well as long term.

However, all this is premised on the assumption that the player will *want* to engage in the loops to begin with. If the loops are not interesting to the player, they will not want to play the game and they will not enjoy our elegantly designed machine.

So, what is it that motivates players to play our game? In chapter 2, "Player Experience," we already talked about large-scale player motivations—the desire for particular types of experience, such as challenge, strategy, or community. We also talked about how personality types might affect what players enjoy and how to take all of this knowledge into account in overall game design.

In this section, we turn our attention to small-scale motivation: what motivates players to play the game on a minute-by-minute or hour-by-hour basis and the shared psychological principles behind it.

### Intrinsic and Extrinsic Motivation

First, we can talk about two broad types of motivation.

- *Intrinsic motivation:* when the player is inherently interested in the activity and its outcome. In this case, there is something about the activity that the player finds appealing—for example, dancing in *Dance Dance Revolution* or learning to fly around the world in *Microsoft Flight Simulator* may be intrinsically enjoyable.

- *Extrinsic motivation:* when the player is driven by sources external to the activity, such as by desiring just the outcome but not necessarily the activity itself. Grinding to get great items or competing in a match to get the top prize may be examples of being motivated extrinsically.

These types of motivations are not exclusive and most activities fit somewhere on the spectrum between being intrinsically and extrinsically motivated. For example, an activity like playing a competitive multiplayer game usually mixes goal-driven motivation (getting a top position on the leaderboard) with some intrinsic pleasure of the game itself. Similarly, a racing game can combine the intrinsic rush of driving quickly and effortlessly with the extrinsic reward of competing for the top prize in a race, both of which are rewarding in different ways (Hodent 2017, 65).

The details of intrinsic and extrinsic motivations are specific to particular players. Looking from the outside, we cannot tell how much someone is playing to get a reward, or playing for the enjoyment of it, or some combination of both. So, although a game cannot shape a player's intrinsic motivation, it should *support it* whenever possible. We cannot make the player enjoy dancing in a virtual competition in *Dance Dance Revolution*—this motivation has to come from within. But if they do, or they think they do, we can build a scaffolding that will make them grow in skill and enjoyment.

On the other hand, extrinsic motivations are easier to manage artificially. Getting more points, getting a high score or a cash reward, winning in a competition against others—these kinds of motivations are popular across many types of games. They speak to the more basic human desires to get better, to compare ourselves against others, and to see the rewards of hard work.

Ideally, games combine intrinsic and extrinsic motivations. A game that provides extrinsic rewards but is not itself interesting is going to turn into a job. On the other hand, an activity that is enjoyable but does not provide feedback about performance or some extrinsic rewards might feel too undirected and "loose" for some types of players. Games are most widely approachable if they can both fulfill the player's intrinsic desire for a specific kind of activity with the extrinsic "carrot" that also rewards them for getting better and better at what they already enjoy intrinsically.

**Intrinsic Motivation: Flow and Learning**

What is it that makes players interested in a game? Why do they enjoy engaging with it repeatedly, minute after minute and hour after hour? Everybody has their own reasons and motivations, but there are some commonalities that are broadly shared.

In this section we focus on the idea that gaining mastery of a skill or a domain is inherently interesting to players and serves as a powerful motivation behind our desire to play. Reaction to challenges is not the same across all players. It is based very much on where we are mentally when we encounter the particular challenge, whether we are able to meet the challenge, or if we are improving and learning from it. But even so, we as humans find learning and mastering challenges to be intrinsically interesting if it matches our interests and skill levels.

Surprisingly, this interest in a challenge is true regardless of whether the challenges are useful life skills or "useless" pastimes such as video games. The connection between ability and mastery on one hand and games on the other has been noted since the earliest theoretical writings on games (Caillois 1962).

**Flow Theory**

The concept of *flow* is central to understanding the joy of mastery. Commonly it is described as the feeling of "getting into the zone" when doing something. Anyone who has gotten lost in a game or an activity for hours at a time and not realized how much time had passed has experienced that intense, euphoric feeling.

People who get "into the zone" often report similar psychological effects, losing track of time being the most common one, as well as hyper focus on the single task at hand and losing track of oneself and one's presence in the world. When we are in the zone, it is just us interacting with the activity without anything getting in the way. This effect can happen in a variety of contexts: mental challenges, creative activities, as well as with physical challenges such as with athletes pushing themselves beyond their skill level.

The psychological theory of flow posits that getting absorbed in activity like that is tied directly to the person's skill and how well the challenge of the activity matches this skill (Csikszentmihalyi, Abuhamdeh and Nakamura 2005). If the activity is too easy the person will be bored, and when it is too hard, they will get frustrated or anxious. But if the subject is focused on the task and challenged well for their skill level, they will enter an optimal kind of state where they are fully engaged with the activity, as illustrated in figure 5.8.

Csikszentmihalyi et al. (2005) postulate three core conditions of getting into the flow state.

1. A *clear set of goals* that channel attention towards specific purposes
2. *Balance* between perceived challenges and user's perceived skills in order to absorb one's attention into the task
3. Clear and immediate *feedback*, which tells the person how to adjust their actions

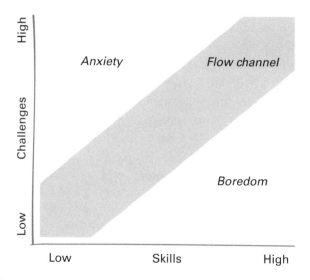

**Figure 5.8**
Illustration of the player's flow channel in which the challenge level is correctly balanced against player's skill level

They also mention in passing one more optional element that supports getting into the flow state: *congruence* between task-specific goals and longer-term, more abstract goals.

For players, this state of flow is highly desirable and games often actively trigger it. As we have seen, games employ a variety of techniques to satisfy conditions 1, 3, and 4. Game content and the variety of systems provide a large variety of clear and actionable goals for the player to choose from at different scales and frequencies which are set up to support each other. Also, feedback on how well the player did is plentiful, including using progression mechanics to guide the player along.

But one thing that games cannot easily do by themselves is balancing the challenge to match the player's skill. This is something that is still a difficult design challenge. Most often, we resolve it by having the player pick their "difficulty level," but that is often unsatisfactory (the player does not know or care to adjust the difficulty level correctly and will not experience the right level of challenge).

In multiplayer games, the problem seems easier. We may try to match the player automatically against an opponent of similar skill, using scores or Elo ranking as proxy for skill measurement. This works well over a longer period of time, but is harder to tune correctly for new players. Many multiplayer games suffer from a "learning cliff" (as opposed to a learning curve) during which brand new players do not get correctly matched and are expected to accept a period of frustrating losses as a part of the learning experience.

In the end, reaching the feeling of flow is central to successful gameplay. It requires the whole variety of game building blocks to work together—mechanics and systems that provide challenges for the player, systems and content that gives them goals, and finally the enjoyment of interacting with all of these elements and getting a good experience out of the challenge, exploration, and experimentation.

### Learning and Challenge Escalation

Koster's *A Theory of Fun* (2004) presents a related but slightly different argument. He posits that the enjoyment or "fun" of playing a game comes from learning, from acquiring mastery of activities in the game, and especially acquiring the skill to *predict outcomes* within the game. For example, this might mean learning how to navigate a particularly tricky level or figuring out how to solve a given type of a challenge or perhaps following a narrative and figuring out what will happen next. Additionally, this learning must happen in a safe environment in which stakes are low but challenges are still interesting so that the player has room to experiment and have fun while learning.

This model comes from a different perspective than flow theory (from the intuition of game design practitioners rather than from psychological studies), but it reaches similar conclusions: that enjoyment arises out of learning, out of understanding how something works, and out of having the space to figure it out.

But if learning how to predict or "figure out" the game is part of the fun, what happens once the player figures it out? One implicit consequence is that if a game has static or limited content, the gameplay will inevitably become boring once the player learns it and is able to predict how the game will behave. In the context of the previous discussion of loops and activities, this motivates why we need multiple gameplay loops at different frequencies as well as content arcs that modulate those loops. Once the player learns the small loops quickly, they will no longer hold any secrets. To keep the player engaged, we need to vary them. For example, repeat smaller loops but escalate them (such as by matching the player up against increasingly advanced opponents), stack on larger loops that are more difficult (as with systems-heavy games), or perhaps stack on loops that present very different challenges (such as adding a long-term narrative arc).

The major difficulty here is that the player's knowledge and skill keep increasing, so we need to keep the loops carefully in sync with player's changing skill. If the challenge jumps too quickly, this may end up being frustrating, and although some players like this kind of a feeling, others hate it. Conversely, if the challenge increases slower than skill, the game may be too relaxed and ultimately boring, and, again, some players enjoy relaxing activities that are below their skill level and others are infuriated by them. And sometimes the same player might have both reactions to different kinds of activities within the same game, depending on their mood or goals (whether they want to be challenged or relaxed).

## Learning to Overcome Uncertainty

We have said that learning and skill mastery are crucial to enjoyment, and Koster argues that learning is intrinsically fun. This seems intuitive but with a caveat—clearly not all types of learning are equally fun. We can easily come

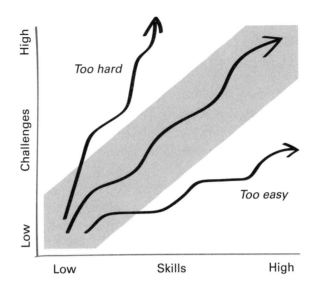

**Figure 5.9**
Examples of activities that leave the flow channel owing to presenting too much challenge or not enough challenge for the skill level

up with counterexamples, such as a game oriented around learning mathematics or mastering a foreign language. Though the activity could be challenging and motivating, would we say that learning math is fun *as a game?*

Costikyan's *Uncertainty in Games* (2013) argues that learning is not enough and that one unique characteristic of games is that they are frameworks for *learning how to manage uncertainty*. When we play sports or esports, we slowly learn how to control our own movement and attention. In sports as well as in *chess*, we learn how to anticipate what our opponents will do. In racing or strategy games, we learn how to analyze and anticipate the behavior of a complex mechanical system. The behavior of these systems is uncertain, and we enjoy figuring out how they work and how to control them in a play environment that supports trying, failing, and experimenting.

Costikyan's taxonomy enumerates the following major and minor types of uncertainty.

- *Randomness:* dealing with an unpredictable random process, like dice or a deck of cards. Knowing your odds at the blackjack table or figuring out where you might land with the next dice roll in *Monopoly* are some examples of why reasoning about randomness is crucial. Randomness is a very common kind of uncertainty, easy to introduce into various game rules, and an easy way to introduce dramatic tension and "shake up" predictable gameplay. In chapter 3, "Mechanics," we discussed two types of randomness: stationary randomness like die rolls and nonstationary randomness like a shuffled deck of cards. These challenge players in different ways, testing their understanding of probability distributions and their ability to predict future outcomes from a history of previous ones.

- *Skill uncertainty:* not being able to act as one intends and training or learning to overcome it. Inability to act is a big source of uncertainty and negative emotions for new players, but it decreases as they learn how to play the game. Overcoming skill uncertainty is often required to attain mastery at a particular game or sport. Since the player's own ability is the source of uncertainty, we can increase or decrease it by changing the game's difficulty or challenging the player's ability to train and learn. We can consider them as three sub-types:

  - *Performance uncertainty:* the player has difficulty performing the tasks with skill or precision. Action games or sports that require the player to train to get good are a good example.

  - *Perception uncertainty:* the player has difficulty seeing or sensing what they need. Games with overwhelming or subtle displays, from RTS games on one hand to hidden objects games on the other, are examples.

  - *Solver's uncertainty:* the player has difficulty identifying the right solution to the problem at hand. Puzzle games, whether casual crosswords or more involved adventure games, exceed at this kind of uncertainty.

- *Player unpredictability:* not knowing what your opponents will do. This is a significant source of uncertainty in multiplayer games, since the player does not know what the enemies or collaborators will do, and learning to figure them out is a major challenge and a strategic advantage. This is present in a variety of multiplayer games as well as sports. Player unpredictability also applies when the other player is a computer-controlled AI character or gameplay system (for example, friendly and unfriendly nonplayer characters). The challenge is similar: the player is challenged to figure out how the AI works in order to improve their chances of success.

- *Complexity:* dealing with situations that are hard to figure out. This kind of uncertainty is common in strategy games: *chess*, war games, management games, and others along these lines. We can distinguish two types:

- *Analytic complexity:* reasoning about the current game state taxes the player's mental abilities. This is very common for games with large action spaces and states with high branching factor, such as **chess** or war games, or games that exhibit emergent or chaotic behavior. Analytically complex games tax the player's ability to infer the future from the present, and this kind of uncertainty can be improved by letting the players experiment, explore, and slowly build up a mental model of how the world works.

- *Hidden information:* the player is missing all the data they need to make a good decision, such as in strategy games that employ fog of war or games like *poker.*

- *Anticipation:* trying to anticipate what happens next in the overall game. Sometimes the uncertainty comes simply from not knowing what the designer has in store for us. With this kind of uncertainty, players will be challenged to prepare themselves for whatever might happen next at the whim of the designer. Players often enjoy anticipating the future and then seeing how their predictions turned out and if they were able to prepare accordingly. This level of uncertainty can be modulated by keeping the changes reasonable within the logic of the game universe and giving players appropriate clues about how things are going to change over time. We can distinguish three subtypes:

  - *Narrative anticipation:* the player does not know what comes next in the story so their ability to prepare will be challenged. This is particularly common in story-driven games where the player's trajectory through the game is deliberately full of interesting turns.

  - *Game evolution:* the game simply changes over time and challenges players to prepare. This is common with games such as *Magic the Gathering* or social games such as *CityVille*, as well as esports games like *Hearthstone*, in which the game is guaranteed to evolve and players need to anticipate it to keep up with their friends or competitors.

  - *Real life uncertainty:* the game challenges players to adjust their real life to the demands of the game in order to advance and win. This is common in games with significant multiplayer elements, such as MMOs, esports, or other competitive multiplayer types in which participation in guild raids, scheduled competitions, and other such activities impact players' real-life schedules.

The various types of uncertainty are used to challenge the player and make this challenge enjoyable. Games often employ multiple types of uncertainty at the same time—for example, a CCG like *Magic the Gathering* might interleave random processes (cards), hidden information, player unpredictability, high amounts of analytic complexity (arising from the complex combat and resource mechanics), as well as significant game evolution and real-life uncertainty elements.

### Dominant Strategies and "Solving the Game"

Just like "enjoyment," the player's feeling of challenge is also subjective and based on their previous experience. Children like to play *tic-tac-toe* because it challenges their ability to analytically predict how it will unfold. But for adults, the game holds no secrets—and without that uncertainty, the enjoyment is also gone. A challenge that becomes predictable and rote loses a lot of its appeal.

Enjoyment of a challenge sits in the peculiar valley between full unpredictability and full predictability. If a game is completely unpredictable, like *roulette* or other games of chance, that reduces the enjoyment coming from gameplay (although players may still play for different reasons, like the thrill of gambling one's money on a lucky draw). Conversely, if the game is predictable, it also loses appeal, for the opposite reason—if we already know how it will turn out, why even play?

To ward off predictability, designers pay special attention to *dominant strategies* in games, strategies which clearly bring out better results than others. A simple example of a dominant strategy in *tic-tac-toe* is to start the game by putting the first mark in the center of the board rather than somewhere else, which guarantees that any opponent moves can be countered and each game can be won or tied but not lost.

Dominant strategies can also be subtler. For example, when the game *Civilization V* first came out, different civilizations had different unique buffs, but the French civilization had a particularly powerful buff that allowed them faster border expansion compared to others. Playing as the French and concentrating on specific upgrades early on, one could easily outgrow other empires mid-game, which then led to easy victory. (As expected, this unbalanced tuning got viciously nerfed in a subsequent expansion pack.)

Dominant strategies affect enjoyment of a challenge, but they are difficult to find analytically. Finding them typically involves a lot of playtesting before the release, as well as adding analytics to games after the release and monitoring for specific patterns of play that cause unexpected scores or win ratios.

### Loops and Challenges

Do smaller loops always offer smaller challenges? As we have already hinted, this is not necessarily the case. For example, in action games participating in the micro loop starts out difficult. Driving the car while passing and not crashing, shooting at alien space ships while avoiding their missiles—these take a lot of practice to get good at them. Arcade games, from *Space Invaders* or *Asteroids* to the more recent *Flappy Bird*, made punishingly difficult micro loops their hallmark. In comparison, larger loops in these games are easier (or nonexistent) and participating in them is a more abstract, aspirational goal for more advanced players.

We see the opposite in strategy games or board games. The more strategically oriented the game, the easier the micro loop tends to be, as moving pieces on the game board can be tedious or require some calculations but is not typically meant to be challenging. The larger challenge is in the medium- and long-term strategy of knowing what should be moved, where to allocate resources, and how to play the long game.

Games are likely to mix the two approaches. For example, squad-based tactical FPS games such as the *Call of Duty* series mix challenging micro loops that demand physical dexterity and fast reaction times with longer term loops based on the tactical situation of the entire squad as well as a solid amount of metagame.

Figure 5.10 illustrates this situation using onion diagrams based on an example from Koster (2012).

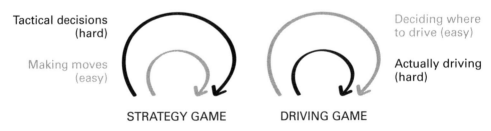

Tactical decisions (hard)

Making moves (easy)

STRATEGY GAME

Deciding where to drive (easy)

Actually driving (hard)

DRIVING GAME

**Figure 5.10**
In some games the small loops are more challenging than the large loops, but in other games it is the opposite, after (Koster 2012)

## Extrinsic Motivation: Work and Rewards

So far, we have focused on intrinsic motivation coming from internal enjoyment of the activity. In contrast, when the player is driven by the *outcome* of the activity, such as rewards or acclaim, rather than the activity itself, we can say that they are motivated extrinsically. These kinds of motivations are also common in games and supported by progression mechanics as well as other game design elements.

Here we introduce some ways in which players find extrinsic rewards motivating and what games do to support them and to tie extrinsic and intrinsic motivations together.

### Progression and Rewards

It is very common for games to reward progression with achievements and leaderboards. Many platforms (including consoles or the Steam desktop platform) support them natively and make it easy for the player to see their virtual trophy wall or score board and maybe even show it off to other players.

The family of *progression mechanics* includes these kinds of rewards. These mechanics encompass the different ways for giving the player feedback on their progress. As discussed previously in chapter 3, "Mechanics," these are elements such as:

- *Score* or *XP* (increases as the player accomplishes various goals)
- *Levels* (earned as the player reaches specific milestones)
- *Achievements* (earned for reaching specific uncommon goals)
- *Leaderboards* (show how players' scores, levels, etc., stack up against those of other players)

Progression mechanics can provide a variety of extrinsic goals for players. They are very commonly used in games because they provide that extra bit of motivation. As the player's intrinsic motivation tends to wax and wane over time, the additional extrinsic "carrot" helps to tide them over. Additionally, the rewards themselves can be enjoyable on a meta level. For example, getting a high score can bring acclaim and jealousy among friends.

Some mechanics can also serve a double duty as rewards in addition to their regular role. For example, amassing cash, gold, resources, or units can provide feedback about one's progress and feel like a reward separately from how those resources can be used later in the game. Similarly, the game's developing story can be interesting by itself and also give the player a sense of their progress.

However, it is important to note that extrinsic rewards by themselves are not sufficient to make a game enjoyable. They provide motivation, but the game activities have to be enjoyable for the player as well.

**Reward Schedules**

Assuming that we grant extrinsic rewards, we should consider *when* to do so. What is the best way to grant them to the player? At what kind of pace, or based on how much effort? What will be the most appealing to players?

To answer questions like these, we can turn to psychological studies of rewards and of how rewards motivate people in general, not just in context of games. One widely known group of approaches is *operant conditioning*, which is the study of how different types of predictable rewards (or punishments) affect behavior.[12]

For example, in some classic experiments, handlers would teach a pigeon to peck at a marked target spot and get food as a reward, and then they would vary how often the rewards get dropped to see if that affected the pigeon's motivation and persistence. The term *reward schedule* describes a particular plan for how rewards get generated over time based on some chosen principles (for a simple example, we could give out one unit of food every five pecks, or one unit of food every minute).

It is commonly known that animals can usually be trained to do simple things for food, but one of the discoveries was that specific kinds of reward schedules would result in very different training results, some better than others. Another interesting discovery was that by spacing out the rewards, subjects could be trained to do increasing amounts of work in exchange for their rewards (up to a point where they lose interest).

Since its heyday in the middle of the 20th century, conditioning has been *thoroughly* criticized in psychology and education as a massively

---

12. Other types of conditioning also exist. For example, *classic conditioning* studies how events that co-occur become associated together in the subject's mind, such as the famous example of dogs learning to associate the sound of a bell with an imminent meal. We do not address them here, but please see (Hodent 2017) for more details and examples.

reductionist and inadequate view of human learning or motivation. This criticism is fitting. There is much more to human behavior than learning from rewards. We are intelligent creatures and our motivations are complex. But even so, reinforcing behavior through rewards does work on us even if in limited ways.

In game design, reinforcement and reward schedules are very commonly used, although not without controversy. They are criticized for encouraging players to focus on extrinsic rewards over their intrinsic motivations (Hodent 2017, 61–66) or for being overtly manipulative. Some critics also raise a moral panic, accusing them of exploiting human weaknesses for corporate profit and comparing them to gambling (Juul 2010).

However, virtually all video games use extrinsic rewards, and most commonly they use variable ratio schedules (described next) because they work very well in motivating the player. It is useful to understand how they work and how they are limited so that we can use them in positive ways.

### Types of Schedules

Many kinds of reward schedules have been studied, but the basic schedules we will discuss here are as follows:

- *Continuous:* reward the subject for each action directly
- *Fixed interval:* reward the subject every $n$ seconds while they are performing actions
- *Fixed ratio:* reward the subject every $n$ actions
- *Variable interval:* reward the subject at randomized points in time while performing actions
- *Variable ratio:* reward the subject every randomized number of actions

These schedules can be compared based on two criteria:

- *Response rate:* how many actions are performed over time, or in other words, how hard the subject is "working" to get their rewards
- *Resistance to extinction:* how long does the subject keep performing actions and waiting for rewards even if those rewards are no longer coming

The results are startlingly consistent across different experiments and subject types. Results of how trained animal subjects perform can be summarized in a chart in figure 5.11. Lines represent subject actions, and dots represent rewards.

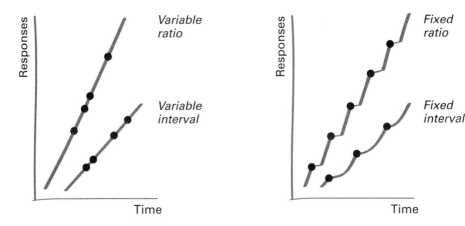

**Figure 5.11**
Response rates of different reward schedules, patterned after Walker (1975, 81). Lines represent subject actions; dots represent rewards.

To describe these results in more detail, here is how the schedules stack up with the most effective schedule first.

*Variable ratio:* for example, reward the pigeon for pecking but vary how many actions are required for a reward. Maybe pecking ten times triggers the first reward, the next one after twenty times, then down to five, and so on. This ratio has the highest response rate (the pigeon works the hardest) and slowest extinction rate (it takes longer for the pigeon to give up) than other schedules. It rewards the subject's active participation, and the variable schedule teaches the subject to not give up too quickly if the rewards are not coming for a while.[13]

*Variable interval:* reward the pigeon for time spent pecking, but vary the time delay between rewards. Maybe sometimes ten seconds of pecking will be enough for a reward, at other times fifteen or twenty seconds. This reward is tied to randomized time intervals rather than amount of work, and it also results in slow extinction (the pigeon does not give up

13. There also exists a related *random ratio* schedule, in which each action may be rewarded separately based on random chance, such as the roll of dice rather than randomizing the total number of required actions. This schedule is commonly seen in gambling, such as slot machines (Schüll 2012, 344). However, this distinction is subtle and the two schedules are similar enough for our purposes, so we will use "variable ratio" as a shortcut for both.

easily) but less work per unit of time (the pigeon does not work as hard), since the reward is not tied to the level of activity.

*Fixed ratio:* reward the pigeon every twenty pecks. With rewards spaced out predictably based on the amount of activity, the activity level is good but extinction is faster (the pigeon gives up when the reward stops coming). Also, it is more likely that activity will slow down right after a reward.

*Fixed interval:* reward the pigeon every twenty seconds if it keeps pecking. Giving out rewards on a steady schedule shows faster extinction and lower reinforcement (pigeon does not work hard). Also, work slows down after a reward but then speeds up as expected reward time approaches.

*Continuous schedule:* reward the pigeon with every peck. This schedule (not shown on the chart), has the fastest extinction and lowest reinforcement of the set, as subjects get satiated quickly and lose interest if the rewards stop.

Although these results are best known from animal studies, they have been repeated in various ways across a variety of test subjects including humans. Something about the anticipation of a somewhat unpredictable future reward has clear effect on human and animal subjects alike, and variable schedules are especially good at teaching their subject not to give up even if their reward is not forthcoming.

## Game Examples

To see how reward schedules can be successfully used in games, let's go back to our ongoing example of dungeon crawlers—and specifically, games from the *Diablo* series.

The core loop is that we go out and kill monsters, collect loot, come back to camp, and sell loot. Loot is collected after combat. Monsters randomly drop loot and gold when killed. Levels also contain scattered treasure chests with random loot. Additionally, there are different types of loot. Tougher monsters drop better loot on average, and both monsters and chests also occasionally drop rare, collectible items.

If we consider combat as "work" (i.e., successfully finding and killing monsters over time), we can see that loot is a reward for this work. But what kind of a reward schedule is it on?

Monsters take a randomized amount of work to kill and upon success they drop a randomized amount of reward, which is proportional to how tough the monster was. This is a variable ratio reward schedule: rewarding the player for their actions with some built-in randomness, the details of which are opaque to the player.

Sometimes monsters also drop rare collectibles that have much higher value, more like rare payouts from slot machines. This is a secondary reward schedule layered on the first one. It is also a variable ratio schedule, like the first one but with much higher payouts for much higher amounts of work.

But combat is not the only way to get treasure: you can also explore to find treasure chests. Various locations hide treasure chests that drop different types of loot than monsters do. This requires finding those treasure chests, which in turn requires exploration and risk-taking (like fighting monsters along the way), and it might also require extra skills or tools to open them. Just like with monsters, the drops follow a variable ratio schedule but in exchange for a different type of activity.

Similar to monsters, some chests randomly contain very high value drops, so they also have a secondary variable ratio schedule layered on top, one that is slower but with much higher rewards.

So, in summary, this dungeon crawler loop employs four different reward schedules.

### Rewarding combat

- High-frequency variable ratio
- Low-frequency variable ratio

### Rewarding exploration and risk taking

- High-frequency variable ratio
- Low-frequency variable ratio

Interestingly, combat loops and exploration loops have their own multiple-reward schedules, and they are tuned differently to keep things interesting and unpredictable. This is a great example of chaining multiple concurrent types of schedules to reward the player for both varying their activity and also for advancing their skills in all of them.

### Changing Workload

Another aspect of reinforced behavior is that, once learned, it can become a basis for new kinds of behaviors—either more complex work or a higher workload for the same kind of a reward.

**Loot boxes.** A recent controversy in game development is the use of loot boxes, which are surprise "treasure chests" that the player can buy with real money, or sometimes earn through playing. Each loot box contains some number of randomized rewards, a combination of low-value ones along with a chance of getting a rare or high-value reward.

These treasure chests have been criticized for being dangerously like gambling. First, loot boxes are perfect examples of random ratio reward scheduling in which the player puts in "work" for a random chance of getting one of the rare items, which is a behavior with high reinforcement and low extinction rates. Second, the "work" usually boils down to spending real money for each chance to open a new loot box, which can lead to excessive spending and other problems associated with compulsive behavior.

Multiple countries are already investigating or regulating loot boxes based on their similarity to gambling. How this might affect the use of variable ratio rewards in games in general remains to be seen.

This effect is intuitively known by teachers and trainers. Teach the student something simple and reward them consistently, and once that is mastered, you can start increasing how much they have to work for the reward (for example, to build up endurance) or you can use that as a building block to make the work more complex (for example, by adding more complications).

This is commonly done in games as well. Perhaps most typical example are *level curves*, which are the formulas for how character experience points (XP) translate into increases in character level. In many games, a player earns XP through in-game actions, such as killing monsters or exploring areas and collecting items. Characters also have levels which increase upon reaching appropriate XP milestones and unlock new abilities and rewards. And very often, those milestones are not spaced out evenly but require ever-increasing amounts of XP to reach.

For an example, consider the following XP/level chart for *Diablo III*, summarized in table 5.2.[14] It shows a very typical, sharply increasing level curve, similar to what can be observed in many games.

---

14. Although this particular data has been contributed by the community of players and can contain inaccuracies in the specific values, the general shape of the level curve is characteristic of games of this type.

**Table 5.2**
XP/leveling chart for *Diablo III*

| Character level | XP required to reach level |
|---|---|
| 1 | 0 |
| 2 | 280 |
| 3 | 2,700 |
| 4 | 4,500 |
| 5 | 6,600 |
| ... | |
| 10 | 19,200 |
| ... | |
| 20 | 57,200 |
| ... | |
| 30 | 115,200 |
| ... | |
| 40 | 420,000 |
| ... | |
| 50 | 2,080,000 |

*Source*: Excerpted from DiabloWiki (2018)

In a level curve like this, every time we reach a new level, the XP required to reach the next level also increases. This has an interesting effect on the player—they have to either work harder to get the next reward or they have to work smarter to get more XP with the same amount of work (for example, by crafting better weapons or finding more profitable enemies). In some cases, this might make them want to play the game more, but in others the increasing amount of work will demotivate them, depending entirely on the combination of how the rewards were tuned and the player's own motivations.

### Related Topic: Gamification

Gamification is closely related to extrinsic rewards. It is the application of progression mechanics to domains outside of games. For example, online discussion boards like Stack Overflow reward participants for their contributions with points and badges and eventually level-based ability unlocks (that is, the user needs a high enough score to be able to post new questions).

Since gamification provides extrinsic rewards, it can definitely serve as a "carrot" to drive desirable behavior but with caveats. First, the reward needs to be meaningful and valuable to the participant. Leveling up to unlock a new ability is more meaningful than leveling up and merely getting a higher number in the player's profile. Secondly, the activity itself needs to be interesting as well. Just getting points without enjoying the activity behind it is neither interesting nor meaningful. A chore is still a chore even if you add points to it, and a leaderboard for who gets the most points is still a leaderboard for chores. Rewards do not drive motivation just by themselves.

## Gameplay Loop Design Heuristics

Let's say we have an idea for a game, and we even worked out roughly what the player is going to be doing and what kinds of experience they will be having. Now we want to figure out how to design the gameplay loops that will drive it. How do we get started?

At the end of chapter 4, "Systems," we talked about using user stories to guide system design. This technique of starting with *user stories* is broadly useful, and we can use it to guide gameplay loop design as well.

### From User Stories to Gameplay Loops

Consider our previous example involving a tower defense game. We can start by asking, "what will the player be doing over and over again?" Can we find a core loop just from a narrative description?

We can take a stab at it as follows:

Player builds out defenses, then waves of creeps spawn and attack the player's base. Killed creeps drop coins, which can be used to repair the defenses and build better ones, before the next, more powerful wave of creeps comes to attack.

This level of description is good: the player's actions are going to be building, defending, and then buying/upgrading/repairing. This kind of a loop sounds interesting already, and it could be a viable core loop (and playtesting will confirm whether it is engaging enough).

From this description we can also imagine smaller loops, for example:

During defending, creeps drop coins. The player must pay attention and collect them as they drop, otherwise the coins will roll off the game board.

This describes a very fast, reflex-oriented action loop. Is it interesting and enjoyable? That is for the designer to decide from experience or playtesting and potentially replace it with a different one if this one does not work well.

We can imagine larger loops in a similar way, for example:

> Every wave of creeps grows more and more powerful. But the player can spend large numbers of coins on spells that change what creeps get spawned—for example, there could be spells to make them spawn weaker or slower or with a lower attack rate.

Now this describes a potential long-term loop, which lets the player strategize. If they built up a lot of attack towers, for example, they might want to invest in a spell that makes the creeps weaker to make their tower specialization even more useful. And since the coin cost is high, this is a long-term plan that needs to be worked towards and prioritized vis-à-vis spending coins on other things such as more towers or necessary repairs.

## Playtesting Loops

Once gameplay loops are designed "on paper," it is very important to implement them as soon as possible and actually see how they feel in real life. The implementation can be *in-game* or as a *stand-alone prototype*, depending on whether the loops interact with other systems or can be separated out.

The reason for immediate implementation is that gameplay loops often feel different live than how they read on paper. Narrative description can easily bias the reader to imagine a different experience, a better experience, than the one actually produced by the implementation. And so, it is important to figure out the actual experience of gameplay quickly before we start layering more loops on top. Skilled designers can sometimes infer some of this live behavior just from experience, but even so, there is no substitute for actual working implementation.

## Summary

With this discussion of gameplay loops, we are finally ready to close the loop on player experience. Here are the key takeaways from this chapter:

- We consider *gameplay* in the light of the dynamic experience of players interacting with the mechanics of the game and with each other and how this interaction evolves over time.

- The basic unit of analysis are *gameplay loops*, which are activities in which players engager repeatedly. Games typically consist of a variety of repeating activities with various challenges and decision points. A *fast* or *small* gameplay loop is one that requires frequent decisions and attention compared to a *slow* or *large* loop in which decisions are less frequent. The *core loop* is the smallest loop that is meaningfully enjoyable to the player in a given game, but commonly it is not the same as the fastest loop.

- Games often use *layers* of loops with different speeds to keep the player engrossed by having to juggle decision making at different time scales. *Onion diagrams* are used to visualize this layering.

- A variety of motivations drives players to participate in these loops. We look broadly at intrinsic and extrinsic motivations.

  - The experience of *flow* and "getting lost in the game" is an important intrinsic motivator, and games are well suited to elicit this experience by providing a layering of challenges, decision points, and feedback. Learning skill mastery and learning how to overcome uncertain game behaviors are other types of strong intrinsic motivators.

  - Players are also motivated extrinsically by rewards such as *progression mechanics* (level ups, rewards, high scores). The relationships between rewards and behavior are well studied in psychology, and the concept of *reward schedules* can be used to understand what kind of extrinsic rewards will produce what kind of participation in gameplay loops.

- Since gameplay loops emerge from players interacting with mechanics and systems, their design is inevitably linked. Like we did with systems design, we can start with user stories and see what kinds of interaction loops and systems emerge from analyzing them.

As we saw, gameplay loops operate on various time scales from seconds to minutes to hours and more. And in the next chapter we turn specifically to those long-term effects to see what kinds of structures emerge when we look at the entire game from start to finish, or even the activity of playing and replaying many sessions over an extended period of time.

## Further Reading

### Gameplay Loops

The topic of gameplay loops is often subsumed under the topic of systems, and more detailed discussion can be found in related books such as *Advanced Game Design* (Sellers 2017).

However, gameplay loops as a standalone concept are well known in game design. Perhaps the earliest preserved mention of them is in "Formal Abstract Design Tools" (Church 1999), and perhaps the earliest mention of onion diagrams is in Will Wright's talk "Lessons in Game Design" (Wright 2003, starting at timestamp 13:30). A more recent discussion in "Loops and Arcs" (Cook 2012) is worth reading for the connection between loops and nonrepeating activities.

### Motivation

For readers interested in the broad topic of player psychology, two books stand out because of their focus on games specifically, with plenty of practical examples and advice: *Getting Gamers* (Madigan 2015) and *The Gamer's Brain* (Hodent 2017).

On the topic of player motivation, we have mentioned in passing that intrinsic and extrinsic motivations are two aspects that can be mixed together and are not binary opposites. There is much more to be said on this topic that is outside of the scope of this text. Readers interested in the psychological perspective can find a good introduction in studies on self-determination theory, for example the work by Ryan and Deci (2000).

On the topic of intrinsic motivation specifically, the theory of flow continues to be a strong influence in game design. For a short research overview please see "Flow" (Csikszentmihalyi, Abuhamdeh and Nakamura 2005) or, for a popular science overview, *Flow: The Psychology of Optimal Experience* (Csikszentmihalyi 1990).

On the topic of extrinsic motivation and reward schedules, any number of psychology textbooks will provide a good introduction, and a great example of one with a free online version is *Learning and Reinforcement* (Walker 1975), or the aforementioned Hodent (2017) text which provides a games-oriented introduction. Also, *Addiction by Design* (Schüll 2012) contains a great analysis of extrinsic rewards from the perspective of gambling and the potential for addiction.

Finally, on the game design theory of fun and the intrinsic joy of learning, Koster's book *A Theory of Fun* (Koster 2004) introduces the topic, and "Theory of Fun: 10 Years Later" (Koster 2012) presents a retrospective and examines lessons learned since the initial publication.

## Individual Exercises

### 5.1. Gameplay Loops
Consider some popular game that you know well, either computer or physical.

a. Draw an onion diagram for that game. Identify as many activity loops with different frequencies as you can.

b. What is the smallest (highest frequency) activity loop where players engage in the same activity over and over again? Now what is the core loop or the smallest loop that is enjoyable even in the absence of larger ones? Is the core loop the same as the smallest activity loop?

### 5.2. Loops and Systems
Consider the game and loops from exercise 5.1. What kinds of game mechanics or systems do the different loops work with? Do different loops share any of those systems?

### 5.3. Flow
Describe your own experience of being "in the zone" while playing a game, whether getting lost in the game for a few minutes or for few hours.

a. What was the game, and what was the activity that was so engrossing?

b. How do you think the game achieved that? List the three core conditions of getting into the flow state and describe whether and how the game fulfilled them.

### 5.4. Fun of Learning
Describe two games you know, one where small loops are harder to learn and another where large loops are harder to learn. In both cases, describe how the enjoyment of the game changes as you learn the "easy" loops. Is it enjoyable to be challenged in a different way by the remaining loops?

### 5.5. Extrinsic Rewards
Describe some game you know well that successfully uses extrinsic rewards on schedules. What are the different kinds of activities that create rewards, and what schedules are being used? Does the game ramp up the workload required to get rewards as the player progresses?

## Group Exercises

### G5.1. Identifying and Changing Loops in a Board Game

In this exercise we will identify game loops in the board game *Settlers of Catan* and explore modifying them. (This exercise assumes you have access to this specific board game. The instructor may suggest substituting a different game in its place.)

a. Play the game *Settlers of Catan* through at least once to remind yourself of gameplay. Then, identify gameplay loops by listing out all the various actions you can take in the game (e.g., trade resource cards, build a settlement, move the robber, etc.) and how frequently you get to perform these actions. Each group member should do their own list separately at first. Then have everybody compare their lists to produce a final list for the entire group.

b. Now identify the longest, least frequent loops and remove them from the game by changing or removing the rules or game elements. For example, you can consider removing the robber piece and soldier cards, removing the ability to build cities, and other infrequent elements. Playtest this variant through at least once.

c. Describe how these changes affected your experience of gameplay. Does this feel the same as playing the original? If not, how is it different?

d. Try to "restore" the game by replacing the low-frequency loops you removed with different ones of your own devising. For each element you removed, find a new replacement that will also operate on a similar timescale. Playtest this variant at least once through as well.

e. Describe how the game feels with this new ruleset compared to your previous variant and compared to the original rules.

To complete the exercise, describe in detail:

f. The loops you identified in the beginning

g. The details of what you removed and how that affected gameplay

h. The details of what you added and how that affected gameplay

# 6 Macrostructure

In previous chapters we discussed gameplay—how we start with some ideas about the desired player experience and then create gameplay that brings this experience about using mechanics and systems as the building blocks. In the process, we introduced some tools for *structuring* gameplay. For example, the idea of gameplay loops running concurrently at different frequencies or the ideas of feedback loops that converge or diverge over time.

In this chapter we discuss the structure of gameplay on an even larger scale. We begin by looking at the overall structure of the *entire game* as a content arc—how the player's experience changes from the beginning, through the mid-game increase in challenge and complexity, to a resolution at the end of the game (if the game does have an end). And since this kind of structure is usually intertwined with the fiction of the game, we will look at fiction and narrative first and discuss content arcs in terms of tension and interest trajectories. We also look at narrative structure specifically and talk about specific common patterns in greater detail, proceeding from linear to nonlinear narratives and how they interact with systems such as quests.

Finally, we zoom out even further and examine the structure of the experience outside of individual game sessions and look at how players use this time to play the metagame (adjust their strategies, change up their team, talk with each other about how to play, trade ideas and resources), which is to say, how they play in between playing.

**Motivating Example: *The Witcher***

*The Witcher* is a series of action RPGs where the player takes on the role of Geralt of Rivia, the titular witcher with superhuman abilities who travels the world as a mercenary for hire. In *The Witcher 3*, Geralt seeks to find

**Figure 6.1**
Screenshot from *The Witcher 3*

and rescue his adopted daughter Ciri and faces escalating challenges as he travels across the various warring kingdoms in the land.

*The Witcher 3* is a highly structured and story-oriented RPG. The game opens with a conflict—news arrives that Ciri is in danger, pursued by otherworldly powers—and tension continues to escalate as the player starts on the search and rescue mission. This rescue is the main storyline of the game, but not the only one, as additional side stories add more detail and color to the world along with challenges and opportunities for the player.

As is common with story-oriented RPGs, the player's identity is already prescribed. Geralt's backstory, place in the world, relationships with Ciri and other people, and so on, are all predetermined, and the player inhabits them and *role-plays* the fantasy of what it would be like to be Geralt living in that story world. This main story and the variety of side stories are written, designed, implemented, and placed in the world for the player to discover, typically expressed as a combination of story cut scenes, story goals, and challenges. In addition to explicit story elements, role-playing games like *The Witcher* also tend to include a variety of story-friendly systems like quests and crafting to support the player's progression through the narrative.

In addition to the main and side stories, *The Witcher 3* also aims to be an *open world* adventure. The player does not have to stick to the story, and the world is full of interesting elements that may be unrelated to the main plot—a variety of places to visit, people to help, dungeons to explore, and so on. The player is free to ignore the story and roam around the game world to discover those elements, which is interesting and satisfying on its own. This openness of the world adds greatly to the player's feeling of freedom and control, makes the world feel much more alive, and lets the player "create their own story."

## Game Fiction

In our example we brought up the idea of game fiction, story, and fantasy. In everyday speech they can be used interchangeably, but in game design they have taken on more strongly differentiated meanings.

Most games present the players with some kind of a *fiction* about the game world and the player's own role in the game. This is the thematic vision, the setting of the game, maybe the background story of the world, and it explains the motivation behind the player's actions in the game. Game fiction helps the player understand why the game world is set up the way it is.

This fiction can vary in complexity and authorial control. On the more complex end we have games like RPGs, which might have a very explicit *story* or *narrative*, which gives the player a very specific identity and role, places them in a specific situation, and unfolds the story as the player goes through the game.

On the less complex end, we have games which present the player with just a general *fantasy*, such as *Rome: Total War* that puts the player in the role of a general, or *The Sims* that puts the player in the role of a "godlike" figure overseeing the lives of little computer people. These games present the player with a role and a setting, but the player's own actions form the unfolding narrative, which can vary drastically from one session to the next.

Then on the far end of this spectrum, some games do not have a guiding fiction at all. For example, abstract formal games like *go* or *Tetris* do not use any game fiction, nor do they need to. But for most games, fiction is a very important aspect of a game's appeal because it helps the player understand their role in the game world, appeals to their interest in the theme or setting, and motivates them.

We will now look specifically at the two broad categories: games with a general fantasy on one hand and games with a structured story on the other. But we should keep in mind that these are not binary opposites, and games can vary in how they approach their fiction.

### Fantasy

Many games have a specific fiction but do not tell a specific story. Games such as *Civilization*, *SimCity*, and *Minecraft* let the player act in the game however they want within the constraints of game rules. The world is completely driven by the players' and AIs' activities and their consequences. Instead of presenting a specific authored story, the game lets the player play it out as they want.

Even though they do not have a set story, these games feature a different, powerful construct: the *fantasy* of who the player is in the game world. *Civilization* offers the fantasy of being the ruler of a powerful empire. *SimCity* features the fantasy of being the mayor of a city full of simulated people. *Minecraft* presents the fantasy of being an explorer, a builder, and a crafter who learns alchemy-like skills for producing novel materials out of what they find in the world.

The fantasy of taking on a specific role is a very powerful player motivator. Players greatly enjoy taking on the role of someone new, experiencing the world through their eyes, and facing their challenges. Perhaps because of this, game fantasies are commonly *aspirational*—offering the player the ability to play as someone they would like to see themselves as being, such as a powerful ruler or a skilled soldier, as many commercial games do. However, even roles which are hardly aspirational can produce an interesting fantasy that engages the player, such as the game *Cart Life* that puts the player in the role of a street food vendor who is barely scraping by and for whom living everyday life is a challenge.

Fantasy provides *context* and *meaning* to the player's actions, which color everything they do. This meaning is so important that a game with the same mechanics but a different fantasy or no fantasy at all will feel very different to players. For example, imagine war games as completely abstract games, stripped of the fantasy. Instead of moving armies on a battlefield map and attacking other armies, the player moves plastic tokens on a plain white grid paper board and bumps into other plastic tokens which then disappear. This game will have identical gameplay but, devoid of the war game fantasy and motivation, it will feel different to the player.

Fantasy and story are not exclusive but rather parts of the same continuum and can coexist within the same title. For example, games like the *Grand Theft Auto* series, offer a rich fantasy of being enmeshed in the urban underworld, as well as a very specific narrative. In contrast, in games like *Civilization*, there is a fantasy but no authored story.

### Story

Game story is a very familiar device. The player plays the game as a character in a specific unfolding narrative that has been authored by the game's writers and designers. In our *Witcher 3* example, the player plays *specifically* as Geralt of Rivia, and his story unfolds in specific ways.

Stories are an abundantly common element in games, and players enjoy participating in unfolding narratives. Storytelling can be accomplished in a variety of ways often mixed together.

### Explicit Narrative and Exposition

- The player can be shown cut-scenes that provide specific story elements
- The game can also include storybooks, bestiaries, or other such devices that fill in the story of the world

### NPC Interactions

- NPCs on the player's team or in the world can hold a scripted conversation, which provides more information about the story
- NPCs can also react to what is going on in the game in prescripted ways that carry the story forward

### Environmental narrative

- Players can take on quests, which will lead them to new unexplored parts of the world or provide them with more background information
- Level design and the way the world is laid out and populated can create an unfolding story as the player moves through it and interacts with it
- Populating an area with evidence of past events (for example, a room with red stains and everything in disarray) is a form of environmental storytelling that lets the player infer past events in the story without resorting to explicit exposition
- Environmental cues such as sounds and music changes can similarly inform the player about what had happened in an area, or foreshadow things to come

## Story and Agency

Stories in games present a common dilemma for authors. In order for a story to play out in a specific way as devised by the author, it must necessarily constrain the player's freedom to do whatever they want. However, this also reduces the player's *agency*, or the ability to interact with the game in the way they want to interact and affect its outcomes.

Player agency is a crucial aspect of games. Players enjoy being able to act intentionally in the game and having the game react to their actions, changing the state of the game. Through this, players learn about how the game world works so that they can improve their chances at affecting the future, or perhaps just to experiment and satiate their curiosity.[15]

However, although generally highly desirable, agency interacts negatively with storytelling and authorial control. And so, games can differ greatly in how much they choose to support it. We can imagine this as a spectrum, ranging from full to minimal support.

At one end we have games which focus on telling a specific story and are willing to tightly control player agency to make it happen—for example, *Choose Your Own Adventure* (CYOA) books and, related to them, adventure games. They excel at telling a specific story but at the cost of drastically curtailing agency. The story is already written, character actions are completely prescribed, and the player's agency is reduced to occasionally coming across *choice points* in the plot and choosing what happens next.

At the other end we have *sandbox* games in which the player has full freedom to experiment and affect the world, and the game responds in turn. This freedom is highly engaging and interesting to the player, but it comes at a price. When we let the player do just about anything, storytelling will suffer. The writer will have a hard time telling the story they want to tell in a world without restrictions where the player can very easily ignore the story and do their own thing or act in ways that contradict the writer's intentions.

In commercial games, stories rarely fall into either extreme and instead occupy the large middle ground. They constrain the player's world such that they still have *some* agency but also reduce it ad hoc when needed. For

---

15. In this discussion we largely follow the idea of agency as first sketched out by Church (1999). We say that players are acting intentionally when they can formulate goals and act purposefully towards those goals. However, more variants of this definition exist, see (Wardrip-Fruin forthcoming) for a detailed discussion.

an example from one popular genre, in open-world RPGs, the player can roam around in a fairly unconstrained way and do as they please, but if they want to participate in the main story or side stories, they must accomplish specific story goals in a specific order that will push the narrative forward. These games also prevent situations that would break the story—for example, by making specific quest NPCs impossible to attack or rob. Table 6.1 explores a few game genres and how they handle this trade-off.

## Consistency

Neither fantasy nor story are strictly necessary. Abstract games such as *sudoku* or *dominoes* lack any fantasy whatsoever, or perhaps the fantasy is weak and irrelevant such as in the case of *go* or *chess*. These games are certainly enjoyable as abstract puzzles for the gameplay they provide.

But when some form of game fiction is present, it should match gameplay design. It is important to achieve a consistency between gameplay and fiction, since gameplay and fiction will reinforce each other, which improves the player's experience.

One of the easiest ways to violate this consistency is to limit player's actions in a way that contradicts the fantasy. For example, if a war game presents the fantasy of being an army general, but the player ends up having to manage every single soldier individually, it makes the player feel like a low-level sergeant rather than a high-level commander. Similarly, when a

**Table 6.1**
Variations in authorial control and player agency across select genres

| Game genres and examples | Authorial control | Player agency |
| --- | --- | --- |
| CYOA-style (*Dragon's Lair*, 1983 version) | Most | Least |
| Visual Novel (*Ace Attorney*) | | |
| Story with minigames (*Dys4ia*) | | |
| Adventure game (*Myst*) | Much | Some |
| Action-adventure (*Tomb Raider*) | | |
| Open-world RPG (*The Witcher*) | Varies | Varies |
| Campaign-based strategy game (*StarCraft*) | | |
| Management game (*Rollercoaster Tycoon*) | Least | Most |
| Sandbox simulation (*The Sims*) | | |
| Esports (*Overwatch*) | | |

**Choice and agency.** Giving the player a freedom of choice is an important part of gameplay, but choice by itself is not quite the same thing as agency. A game supports agency if the player can act intentionally, formulate goals, and act on them. But in order to act towards goals, the player must also understand how their actions affect future outcomes.

For a simple example, we can consider a visual novel in which the player can make story choices, but the results are very unpredictable, so the player does not understand how or whether those choices affect the game. Although this could result in a gripping narrative, from the gameplay perspective it will make the player feel like they have no control and agency in the game world because they cannot form a good mental model of how the game works. This kind of a situation would need to be improved by providing better feedback about the connection between actions and consequent changes in the world.

For an even more extreme example, there are games in which intentional actions are flat out unsupported. Children's luck-based games like *Snakes and Ladders* or the *War* card game, in which the player's actions are completely prescribed by dice rolls and card draws, fit this category. Not being able to act intentionally makes them uninteresting for more experienced players.

superhero game gives the player the ability to fly, but level design contains invisible walls intended to force the player's progression through the level, this makes the player's superpowers feel arbitrarily and capriciously limited, not like superpowers at all.

A different violation is the concept of *ludonarrative dissonance*, attributed to Hocking, which refers to contradiction between gameplay and story. In his example (Hocking 2007), the game *Bioshock* lets the player play as a supporter of one of two factions and make corresponding moral choices during the game. However, as the game progresses, the story comes to a point in which the narrative forces the player to support one specific side—no matter how they played out their role thus far—or to stop playing altogether. This story thus contradicts player's role-playing efforts, rendering them insignificant. For another example (Solarski 2017b), *Halo 4* presents a different dissonance. According to the story, the player is urged to defeat the Didact archnemesis, but this story urgency has no gameplay consequences, so the player can patiently explore the game and master their skills instead of rushing towards the finish line. The mechanics render the story's urgency meaningless.

However, consistency violation *can* be a powerful tool, and it can be used to subvert expectations and produce fascinating new types of gameplay. For example, the *Crusader Kings* series presents, on the surface, the fantasy of being the ruler of a kingdom in the middle ages. However, the player spends most of their effort on small-scale politics—managing a network of vassals, keeping the royal court content, and extending the family's power via royal marriages or alliances. In the process, the player learns about a very different side of what it is like to be a king (less of a military commander and more of an administrator and a manipulator).

## Macrostructure and Content Arcs

We can now turn our attention to the large-scale structure of the game. Whether we make a game based on a story or a game without a story, it is important to consider the overall shape of the player's experience throughout the entire course of playing a game.

Game designers routinely try to ensure that the player's experience is not monotonous but rather changes in interesting ways over the course of playing the game. In a story-based game, this *macrostructure* is often described in terms of plotlines and story arcs. In our *Witcher* example, there is the main story arc that starts out in the middle of a conflict and keeps ratcheting up plotlines and story intensity over the course of the game. On top of that, additional side stories come into view with additional challenges and story elements, as well as some comedic relief and breathing room. Combined, the main story and side stories generate a very dynamic story arc, full of emotional ups and downs, surprises, and challenges.

### The Three-Act Model

We often speak of a game as following an *arc*. The metaphor comes from theatre and literature, and the related *three-act model* for describing the trajectory of a story. The model describes stories as made of the following three stages.

*Setup*: introduces the settings and characters, their motivations, situations, and the main conflicts that will set them on their trajectories

*Buildup*: the main conflict of the story is developed and is brought to a critical point through the actions of the participants

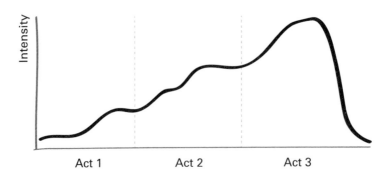

**Figure 6.2**
Intensity of gameplay experience divided into three acts: setup, buildup, and resolution

*Resolution*: the conflict boils over and pushes the settings and characters
    into a new state, thus bringing the story to an end

We could try to graph it in terms of the level of emotional intensity, and
it might look as shown in figure 6.2.

This model has been known since at least the times of Aristotle, and even
though countless authors have extended or transcended it in their own
works, this simple three-act structure persists to this day because it is remark-
ably useful. Something about it speaks to the universal human interest in a
gripping story, escalation of conflict, and seeing how it all resolves in the end.

Interestingly, games without a set narrative exhibit this kind of macrostructure as well. Back in chapter 4, "Systems," we discussed a competitive
multiplayer game like *Monopoly* and saw that that kind of a game also has
its own arc, as players compete and their fortunes rise and fall. The macrostructure of that game is not based on a story but rather based on the
rising intensity of competition as players navigate their way towards the
endgame. Similar arcs are present in other types of games as well.

**Story Arc and Episodes**

Although a movie or a novel can present a stand-alone story, it is also common
to see stories split across multiple parts and presented over time. This is typical
of TV series, sitcoms, serialized novels, comic books, and other such media.

These kinds of stories are *episodic*, meaning individual episodes are tied
together by the overarching narrative. In the short term, each of the short
episodes has its own theme and story, its own ups and downs, conflict
buildup, and resolution. But then added together, they also form into a
larger story that has a larger trajectory of conflicts and denouements.

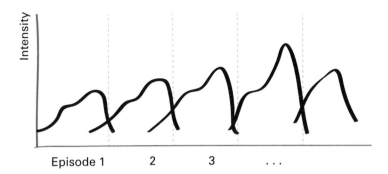

**Figure 6.3**
Episodic experience showing multiple smaller, interweaving act structures

Sometimes this multiepisode narrative is a self-contained story with a large-scale arc structure, for example, when a book is turned into a TV series. But just as commonly, episodes can be designed to form a never-ending narrative like with sitcoms and soap operas, in which case the episodes become a strand of interwoven arcs with new ones always developing and old ones falling out as the series progresses.

We also see episodic arcs in games, especially story-driven games that are divided up into shorter elements. For example, role-playing games (such as *The Witcher* series, *Grand Theft Auto* series, etc.) have their own large-scale story arc or sometimes multiple overlapping arcs that the player follows over the course of many days of gameplay. At the same time, they are divided up into smaller episodes (for example, geographic regions or quest plot lines) which have their own arcs and which take a much shorter time to get through while also advancing the large story arc in the process. As will be mentioned later in the section on pacing, episodes can also help modulate stress and intensity and introduce interesting variety.

Just like TV series have their filler episodes and stand-alone episodes, RPGs also often include optional side quests and open-ended encounters, which can be interesting in themselves and fill in the backstory of the game world but which do not advance the story arc. This gives the player more freedom in the world, since they can pursue side stories and tangential plotlines at their own pace and then come back to the main story when they want to.

We can also see the episodic structure in level-based games from action-adventure games like *Tomb Raider* or FPS games like *Halo* all the way to casual games like *Candy Crush Saga*. Many types of games can be composed of individual levels, each of which has its own short arcs of setup and resolution—but those levels form a sequence with deliberate pacing in which stretches of easier levels are punctuated with harder levels that provide unexpected challenge, variety, and a touch of drama.

### Three-Act Model and Non-story Games

In games without stories, game designers and game players also utilize a three-act model for describing the experience of playing a game. Even in a game like *Civilization* or *chess* it is very common to see non-story gameplay described in terms of how it feels during *early game*, *mid game*, and *late game*. One can see it often in reviews or even casual conversation, "it had a great early game but mid game was too difficult," "late game is poorly tuned and drags interminably," and so on.

This division comes from a common observation that almost every game feels very different at the beginning of playing versus in the middle versus at the end. In sports and competitive games, the beginning is far less intense while there is still room to correct mistakes and mishaps compared to the end game when mistakes are hard to fix. In exploratory games like *Minecraft* or *Terraria*, the beginning is full of exploration and discovery, but over the course of the game, the player transitions to exploiting what they discovered to build fantastic constructions. In RTS games, the beginning is all about figuring out the lay of the land, stashing away resources and building out the base, and preparing for the inevitable showdown with other players, and so on.

We can try to describe these stages as follows:

*Early game* is largely about figuring things out—players explore their situation, figure out the terrain, get themselves situated and started up.

*Mid game* is when things pick up. Players run into challenges with the world or conflicts with each other, and the game becomes more intense, trying to solve challenges posed by the game world, competing over resources, engaging in open or covert conflict, and otherwise work towards winning or achieving one's goals.

*Late game* is when the challenges or conflicts peak and push players toward the resolution of the game (achieving victory or reaching their goals or getting max points, etc.).

These different stages can take on very different shapes depending on the genre. For example, the length can be different. In a war game, the early setup game might take a very long time, and in a physical sports game, the early stage of figuring out your situation can be very short, before the game

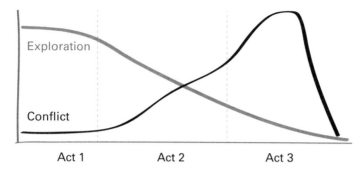

**Figure 6.4**
Example trajectories of exploration and conflict in early, mid, late game in an RTS

is on in full force. Also, intensity can be different. Late game in an RTS might present an intense showdown, but late game in *Monopoly* is infamous for its drawn out, low-intensity war of attrition.

This model applies to single-player games as well as multiplayer ones, since we can replace conflict between players with conflict between the player and AI characters. Similarly, in games without nonplayer characters or without explicit conflict, the intensity of the single player experience will come from having to control and master the unwieldy game simulation or having to face the challenges posed by the game.

## Narrative Patterns

Story-based games use a variety of narrative patterns as building blocks for the overall story arc. In this section we look at these common patterns, first on a smaller scale, and then how these patterns assemble into larger narrative structures. Specifically, we will use structural analysis of the narrative in terms of *choice structure*, how the game interleaves authored story elements with points of player choice which affect how the story unfolds.[16]

Choice is a broad term here. We use it to mean the kinds of decisions, challenges, or actions that the player can undertake that can *alter the course of the story*. Choices and story elements can link together in various ways,

16. Mawhorter et al. (2014) use the term *choice poetics* to describe the analysis of choice topologies and how they interact with other aspects of player experience. The industry does not have a single specific term for this, but terms like *narrative structure* or *story structure* are common.

as we describe next. Some of the basic patterns are illustrated in figure 6.5. These are relatively simple patterns, and smaller games may use them as they are, and larger games may use them as constituents of a larger structure.

**Linear Narrative**

In the simplest case, the story might be completely linear, as shown in figure 6.5a. In classic puzzle-adventure games like *Myst*, the player is faced

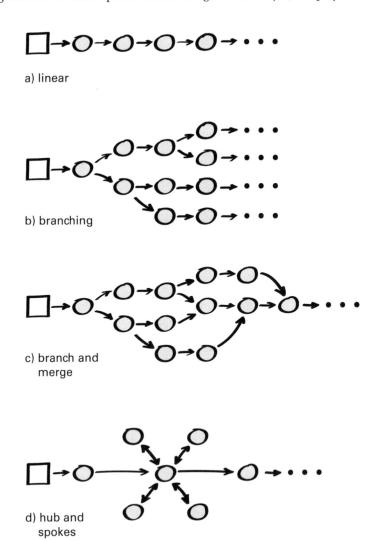

**Figure 6.5**

Examples of popular narrative patterns: a) linear structure, b) branching structure, c) branch-and-merge structure, d) hub-and-spokes structure

with a largely linear, unchangeable story. It might be punctuated with challenges for the player to overcome (puzzles to solve, levels to beat), but the choice points boil down to *succeed* or *fail*. The story is set, and the player must succeed at the current challenge to advance the narrative to the next story point, and the next, and so on.

We see this pattern in other genres as well, such as action-oriented games with a linear progression of levels in which the story is more of a background element that augments gameplay. For example, action games as diverse as *God of War* (the 2005 version) and *Katamari Damacy* tell a great linear background story during interludes between challenging and interesting action levels. Similarly, strategy games like *StarCraft* or *Company of Heroes* often include a "campaign mode" in which various levels are arranged to follow an unfolding preauthored story of a military campaign, and the player must prevail at each step to advance the campaign further.

### Branching Choices

Instead of forcing a linear story, we could give the player choice points which *change* the story in specific, prescribed ways. The popular metaphor for this is one of a *branching choice* structure. The story unfolds one way until hitting a choice point, and then the player's decision can transform the story in one of a few ways. For example, we could give the player choice in a crucial situation to attack an enemy or avoid the fight, venture into the dark cave or find a way around it, and so on. Depending on how the player acts, the story would then follow a selected trajectory (see figure 6.5b).

One of the earliest examples of these games might be the *Choose Your Own Adventure* series of books, which were physical books with numbered paragraphs and each paragraph would tell a bit of the story and then end with either a jump directive (e.g., "turn to page 34") or with a choice point (e.g., "if you choose to attack the monster, turn to page 56, otherwise turn to page 78"). As the player reads the *CYOA* book and makes their choices, the sequencing of paragraphs can produce very different stories on each read-through.

There is one significant problem with this simple branching choice structure: the more choice points we give the player, the more content needs to be authored to make it work across numerous play-throughs so that every single trajectory is equally fulfilling for the player. Written naively, this kind of a branching choice game would suffer from combinatorial explosion of content (Crawford 2005), and explicitly implementing all possible stories that arise from all possible combinations of choices would be impractical for all but the smallest of choice trees. In practice, only small narratives implement this kind of a topology, since it calls for a large amount of content (written story fragments, perhaps voiceovers, animated cut scenes, and so on). Worse yet, a single play-through only explores a *single trajectory* through this space, so most of this painstakingly created content remains unexperienced by the player during a single session.

### Branch and Merge

We can simplify the authoring problem of branching stories by having the branching choices converge periodically, essentially converting a large and bushy tree into a sequence of small and more manageable subtrees. We can call this a "branch and merge" strategy[17] shown in figure 6.5c.

This approach has been criticized for providing choices that are illusory. For example, if the player's choices in the middle of the subtree all lead to the same merge node in the end, are they meaningful "choices"? However, this is an authorial, "bird's eye" view of the topology. In practice, when the player is experiencing the story for the first time, they have no way to know the topology and no reason to think that some of their choices have less impact on the story than others. It is only on subsequent replays that players can start developing a sense for the topology for which of their actions produce what kinds of consequences. However, in story games, there might not be a subsequent replay. The player might be satisfied with the story after playing it once and move on to the next episode or a different game.

Beyond expanding and reconverging, we can list two other choice idioms which may seem suboptimal to authors looking at the topology from above but which often do not reveal their true nature on a single play-through (Mawhorter, et al. 2014). *False choices* occur when seemingly different actions in a choice point both lead to the same next node, although the player does not know that (for example, having different utterances in a dialog tree, all of which will cause the same NPC reaction), while *flavor choices* are similar actions that mainly affect the player's fantasy and perception of the game world (like picking different avatar clothing, or picking a particular turn of

---

17. Costikyan (2007) uses the term "beads on a string" because of how the small subgraphs start from a single choice point, expand into a richer story structure, and then converge back to single point again.

phrase in a dialog). These kinds of choice points can have a strong effect on the player the first time they are encountered without incurring much work, but at the cost of negatively impacting subsequent play-throughs, as the player builds a better mental model of how their actions affect game state.

### Branching with State

Another common development is to add the notion of *state* to the story. Until now, the only data we needed to track was "where is the player in the overall story graph." However, if we also kept track of other data and then used this data to influence choice points, we could produce complex stories from a highly compressed choice graph.

For example, consider how we might implement a conversation, which allows for insults during choice points with the following effect: if you insult someone once, they let it slide the first time, but repeated insults will provoke a reaction in the future. We could try to model it as a pure branching choice structure, but since the player could choose to insult at any number of choice points, the resulting graph would be untenably large. Instead, to implement this example, we can add *conversation state* for insults, which gets incremented every time the player reaches a choice point and decides to insult someone—and then have the story change if that counter goes above some desired value (see figure 6.6).

As we can imagine, adding *game state* that can be modified and queried by the story makes it much easier to express complex relationships between different entities separated by time and space. Beyond single global state, we can also track character stats (health, stamina, etc.), interpersonal relationship (for example representing friendship strength as a number), and so on, and then use them to guide the developing story.

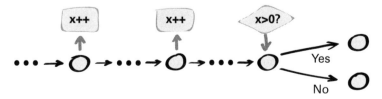

**Figure 6.6**
Example of choice points affecting world state, and future choice point querying world state

Because of its benefits, this kind of approach is *very commonly* used in narrative games, including interactive fiction, adventure games, visual novels, and other similar games. At the same time, this approach greatly increases authorial complexity. Now the author must worry about not just local effects of choice points but also future effects in a variety of different places and times. This kind of "spooky action at a distance" makes debugging potentially much more difficult.

### Hub and Spokes

Instead of pushing the player through a specific sequence of choice points, it might be desirable to give them flexibility instead, perhaps as a collection of choices which all need to be made, but the player can decide in what order and at what time. For example, we could set up a situation where the player needs to speak to some specific character, clear out monsters in a specific area, and produce some artifact, but in any order they choose.

This is commonly referred to as a *hub-and-spokes* pattern. There is a single situation which the player keeps revisiting and some number of story elements are linked to it like spokes in a wheel (see figure 6.5d). The player can go and interact with any element, changing the game state in some specific way, and then return to the hub and move on to another element, and so on.

Compared with the directed acyclic graph approaches we have discussed so far (the linear, branching, or branch-and-merge narratives), the hub-and-spokes approach gives the player more freedom and agency in choosing when and how the narrative will be advanced. Some of the earliest examples of this pattern, such as action-platforming games like *Super Mario 64* and *Jak and Daxter*, embedded this pattern directly in their level design, by having a variety of levels that presented bits of the game world, linked to central hub areas.

### Narrative Composition and Quests

In the previous section we described individual topologies, such as linear, branching, merging, or hub-and-spoke graphs. In some games, these directly describe the overall narrative structure. For example, a *CYOA* game can be modeled as a single branching choice graph. However, for more complex narratives, we may wish to compose them: create small-scale narrative modules using those individual topologies, perhaps implemented as *quests* (sometimes also called *missions*), and then arrange these modules themselves into a larger structure.

A quest in this sense is a short, task-driven narrative sequence, itself usually a small linear or branching structure with specific starting conditions, specific end points that need to be reached, and potentially specific consequences on success or failure. For example, in a role-playing game, the player might meet a *quest-giver* NPC who asks for help getting rid of a ghost haunting the village, which starts a short conversation. If the player accepts the challenge they will end up meeting the ghost, fighting it, and, ideally, coming back in one piece to collect a reward.

Quests are a common and useful storytelling device because they support narrative exposition (such as via cut scenes or NPC dialogue) as well as encourage the player to *participate* in this unfolding narrative, using goals to motivate and completion rewards as a carrot.

A simple composition might be to arrange quests in a linear sequence of areas, each of them a hub-and-spokes pattern (see figure 6.7a) in which each area unlocks after the quests in the previous ones are completed. This is a style used by games like *Jak II*, but it can also be used with narrative elements other than quests. For example, in *Gone Home*, the game requires the player to explore a variety of environmental story elements rather than puzzles in order to advance between hubs.

Composing the narrative by sequencing smaller modules is a good way to scale up the story and allows the designer to build larger narrative structures using smaller, self-contained modules, often via a sequence of quests that can vary greatly and provide much narrative variety.

## Open Worlds

We have already discussed open world games through our example, the *Witcher* series. The open world topology is different still. Instead of having the player follow a chain of elements, the game offers a large collection of various smaller stories, some of which connect together to form the main storylines and some others disconnected (see figure 6.7b). These additional small story lines and narratives are scattered around the world and waiting for the player to discover them. Topologically, we could say the individual stories form a densely connected mesh, since in most cases the player can move from any of them to any other one within their current context (such as based on their character class or level of experience).

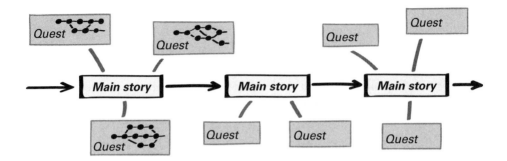

a) linear story with side quests

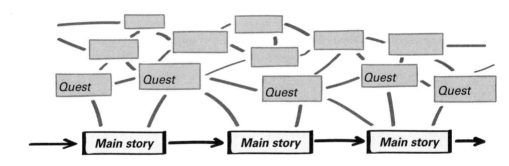

b) open world with a main story and a variety of quests

**Figure 6.7**
Examples of story patterns: a) main story with side quests, b) open world that features a main story plus a variety of quests

Using this model, we can run a variety of story lines and let the player jump in at any time, or leave them aside, explore different parts of the world at their own pace, and generally do whatever they want within the rules of the game. Those extraneous elements may affect their progress along the main story arc, or they might be largely independent, providing some background story, flavor elements, and maybe some boosts or loot drops, and so on.

This control over quests gives the player a lot of freedom and increases their feeling of having agency in the world. It makes open worlds engaging and still pulling the player along a desired content arc (although with much less authorial control over the narrative sequence and pacing).

## Open Worlds and Quest Design

An open world implementation needs to be stateful. Individual characters have persistent state (stats, inventory, etc.), and the world itself has state and remembers what has already happened in the story (which quests got completed, which monsters got hunted, and so on). Some of this state will be visible to the player—for example, they can see their own character's stats and inventory. Other parts of the state will be hidden, such as the game internally tracking which villages have already been visited and which monsters have been slayed, so that it can offer up appropriate quests.

However, as we mentioned before, adding persistent state makes it harder to test and debug created content because it introduces coupling between potentially unrelated parts of the game.

For an extended example, imagine that we are designing an RPG game like *The Witcher 3* and access to specific parts of the game depends on the player having achieved specific milestones in the past. Suppose that one quest early on has the player hunting ghosts in an abandoned village, which increases player's "ghost count" stat. Separately, much later in the game, a special location opens up for ghost hunters once their ghost count meets some desired tuning value.

Now suppose that, many months after both of these quests were written and tested, we come back to iterate on the first quest and decide that it no longer fits the fiction of the early game, that instead of hunting ghosts, we should have the player hunt trolls, and so we tweak the quest fiction accordingly. But this small change might unintentionally damage the late-game secret location, because now the player will not have the means to reach the appropriate ghost count. Worse yet, we may not even notice that we broke the implicit dependency between those two elements unless we were very careful about tracking dependencies between all the various producers and consumers of stats.

Ultimately, it is dangerous to use plain global world state as a communication mechanism between independent content arcs, just like it is dangerous to use global variables in software engineering for communication between different software modules. It enables interesting dependency effects and can be implemented efficiently but also leads to potential for bugs that can be tricky to find and analyze. Because of this, quest-based games often compartmentalize interactions between specific elements to make sure they are not affected by other quests or player actions—and to make any interactions very clear to the designer.

A common technique is to explicitly represent a dependency between two quests as a special *quest item* that is awarded to the player. For example, in *The Witcher 3*, some early quest items are "letters of safe conduct" which unlock access to a new area of the game. These letters are then granted by quest NPCs on completion of specific earlier quests.

In our example case, we could have the "ghost hunter" quest give the player special "entry papers" upon completion and later on have the later area check for their presence. Many months later, when we decide to redesign the "ghost hunter" quest, we will see that it grants a special item, and we can quickly search the codebase for where it gets used. It is also much easier to automate these kinds of checks. If any piece of content produces special quest items, we could have game code verify that at least one other piece of content exists to consume it and vice versa.

In spite of these complications, quest-based open worlds are very popular, and for good reason—they give the player increased autonomy and agency and also provide good control over the content arc and its delivery. Creating open world content is a significant endeavor requiring a lot of authoring and implementation work; but for projects in which that makes sense, they present a sweet spot between agency and authorship.

---

**AI and storytelling.** Stories in games are typically preauthored in the ways described above, with a mix of narrative exposition, heavily scripted quests, situations, and other authored elements. However, there is a growing body of research work around *storytelling AI*, technology to let the player act as they desire and have the game adjust itself to react to those actions such that nevertheless results in storylike outcomes.

This is an open research problem in AI and game design and a formidable challenge in reasoning and knowledge representation. At this point there are no commercial games that attempt it fully, although there are experiments that attempt artificial storytelling in tightly constrained settings. *Façade* (see Mateas and Stern 2003) is probably the best-known example, and is available online.

## Simulated Worlds

At the other end of the spectrum from games with a specific narrative are titles that give the player maximum agency and autonomy—games based on simulation that take player's actions and update the world in reaction to players, AIs, and the rules governing the game world. Genres such as simulation games, strategy games, action-arcade games, and multiplayer games tend to occupy this space.

These games should ideally also follow an arc of variable intensity and a pacing model that provides a variety between tense challenge and relaxation and reflection. However, it is difficult to create predictable content arcs for these games. Players act autonomously within the game world, so their actions are not predictable. In the end, players end up producing their own story and narrative about what happened as they did that.

Without explicit story, we have to rely on setting up gameplay systems, mechanics, and feedback loops, in such a way that a macrostructure arises just from the player's interactions with the game. Systems that create long-term gameplay loops are particularly useful for this purpose.

Some examples of systems that generate long-term arcs include:

- Tech trees or crafting, in which players can spend resources towards unlocking new abilities over an extended period of time and those modulate intensity and challenge. This is very popular in simulation and strategy games, including *Civilization*, *StarCraft*, *Factorio*, and many others.

- Setting up explicit epochs of gameplay tied to specific milestone achievements that unlock new abilities but also present new demands and change the balance of the game. This can provide a very explicit act structure—for example, the four eras of nation-building in *Tropico 5*.

- Adding random events that provide an escalating challenge and possibly some story elements, such as droughts or fires that occur unpredictably and shake up a player's long-term plans. Management games like the *Caesar* series, *Aven Colony*, but also more casual games like *CityVille*, follow this approach.

In the end, setting up long-term gameplay structure for systems-heavy games can be difficult, since designers can only affect player's actions and gameplay indirectly by setting up systems, opportunities, and reward structures in specific ways and then testing to see if things unfold as intended. At the same time, it is important to plan out the macrostructure of these games because players do think of games in terms of early game, mid game, and late game, and how they differ from each other.

## Pacing

As we develop the game's structure, it is important to consider the *pacing* with which the player is experiencing this structure. Pacing routinely refers to the *how the game's intensity varies over time*.

The challenge of pacing is that we need to avoid creating an unrelentingly taxing experience without breaks or respite. Pushing intensity to a high level and keeping it there for a long time is a recipe for mental fatigue, similar to an action movie that is uniformly tense without any chance for the viewer to catch their breath. For example, in level-based shooter games, level designers have long recognized that a relentless onslaught of enemies and challenges ends up being overwhelming and should be avoided. Rather, levels tend to alternate times of high-intensity challenges with quiet areas for the players to have some *downtime* to rest, regroup, or just explore.

The goal of good pacing is to vary gameplay intensity and balance intense gameplay with moments of downtime. How exactly this is implemented varies greatly between genres and game types. For example, in first-person action games, pacing can be achieved through level design by varying amounts and types of threats (such as enemies), mixing safe and threatening environments (such as areas where the player feels exposed and vulnerable), periodically taxing the player's reflexes (such as having to defend against an overwhelming enemy wave), and so on.[18] In other games, pacing can be achieved differently. A turn-based war game still achieves increasing tension by taxing the player's problem-solving abilities rather than reflexes. Games that are not composed of multiple levels but rather consist of one long continuous session (like war games, grand strategy games, or sandbox simulations) also benefit from good pacing by modulating challenge over time. However, this is much more difficult to bring about in systems-driven

---

18. Some games even attempt to automate this. For example, *Left4Dead 2* features an explicit "director" module that tracks the pacing of the game and injects challenges to provide variety (Serviss 2013). However, this particular implementation also attracted player criticism for producing variability that was too predictable, underscoring just how difficult it can be to produce good pacing.

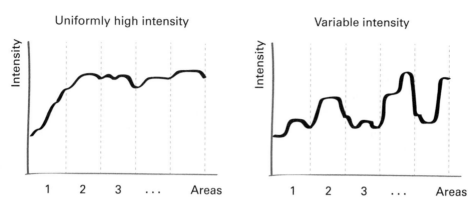

**Figure 6.8**

Example of uniformly high intensity compared to mixing high intensity areas and downtime

games, as it must come out of systems and loops themselves rather than from content authoring.

There are various approaches to adding downtime, reducing intensity, and improving pacing. Most are specific to genres, such as breather levels that are specific to level-based games. But two tactics come to mind that are widely used across different genres: *exploration* and *busywork*.

Exploration is something that the player will do naturally on their own. Players enjoy visiting different parts of the game or experimenting with different mechanics. It is important to leave space in the game for the player to spend some time exploring physically or mechanically, so that they can catch their breath and then return to the main challenge at their own pace.

Alternatively, we can ask the player to do some busywork to advance to their next challenge. This is activity that is time-consuming and *could* be optimized away by the designer, but it forces the player to have some downtime and decompress. For example, having to travel between different quest locations or to spend time on resource gathering can function as busywork (as well as feeding other gameplay systems such as crafting or economy).

However, exploration and busywork generate slightly different player reactions. Exploration is easier to make feel positive, as players typically enjoy learning new things at their own pace. Busywork, in comparison, can easily feel boring, pointless, and ultimately frustrating if it does not provide interesting activity while the player is decompressing between challenges.

## Metagame

In the previous section, we examined long-form games like RPGs, which take many hours to complete, and the kind of macrostructure that supports these kinds of games. But what can we say about short-form games where each session lasts some number of minutes instead? When the individual game sessions are much shorter and simpler, that kind of a game can also exhibit a long-term structure, but structure that becomes evident across *multiple sessions* instead.

For example, in CCGs like *Hearthstone* or *Magic the Gathering*, each session is very short, and, just like in traditional card games, each hand is played and won in a matter of minutes. The tactical challenge (how best to play the hand one's been dealt) is appealing, and having short sessions in quick succession makes for very brisk pacing that leaves the player wanting more.

However, a very interesting structure also happens across multiple sessions. Unlike in traditional card games, players do not draw from the same deck. Instead they bring their own customized decks from which they draw. And so in between sessions players try to figure out how to optimize their decks for each session. They strategize and analyze their opponents, try to figure out what play style would work best for the match, and then add and remove cards to build the best deck for the match. On an even longer timeframe, players discover different card types which might alter their strategy, so they trade cards with other players or spend virtual currency (or real currency) to buy card packs and booster packs that will give them an assortment of additional cards to choose from.

This kind of structure is the *metagame*—the game on top of the game, an enjoyable activity that is based on playing the game but which takes place outside of the individual game sessions or challenges.

We can describe metagame in terms of two popular categories:

- *mastery metagame*, the activity is oriented towards mastering the game, and
- *social metagame*, the activity is oriented towards interacting with others in the context of playing the game.

We will also describe *game modding*, which also happens outside of the game's individual sessions, and lets players use the game as a pliable medium for creative self-expression.

## Mastery Metagame

Sometimes the metagame arises from player's internal motivations when playing the game to improve their skill or to get better at the game. We already discussed CCGs in which players play individual matches and then spend time between matches improving their deck and figuring out what to do next. Other examples might be racing games like *Forza Motorsport* or multiplayer FPS games like *Counter Strike* or *Overwatch*, in which intense game sessions are interweaved with downtime to regroup, perform upgrades, and make other improvements before jumping back in to the next session.

Some popular examples of metagame elements are:

- Performing character or avatar upgrades (ranging from strategic to cosmetic)
- Leveling up character or party members (such as spending level points to upgrade stats)
- Changing inventory and getting new items (cards, weapons, etc.)
- Hiring new party members (or switching cars in a racing game)
- Researching new strategies and analyzing past recordings of sessions

Metagame arises because, in addition to being challenged during each session, the player is also faced with interesting and meaningful decisions *between* sessions. Those decisions are meaningful because they tie back to the systems and mechanics that operate during a game session and they can improve the player's chances of winning or advancing in the game, or they can be meaningful in improving the fantasy, as is the case with cosmetic upgrades.

In games that are not oriented towards winning or competition, we can also see a metagame, but it takes on a slightly different form. For example, in a game like *The Sims*, which is a noncompetitive life simulator in which the player controls one particular family at a time, the metagame might be to build up an entire neighborhood stocked with interesting characters so that interactions between them might lead to more memorable situations and stories.

## Social Metagame

At other times metagame arises because players enjoy the social effects of playing game sessions. For example, when competitive players play together, many short-form games can be turned into competitions—who will get the highest score, who can finish faster, who can perform some unusual move first, and so on. These players will keep replaying game sessions in order to compete and best their friends or get the highest score. This is a kind of a social metagame.

But social metagame does not have to be competitive or adversarial. It can just as easily be creative and collaborative. In the case of *The Sims* or *Roblox*, players can create in-game objects and decorations, upload them to the game website, and get ratings and comments from other players who enjoyed their creation. This is a social metagame as well but is instead based on recognition of work and creativity.

Some more examples of drivers behind social metagame:

- Competing for status as the best player (often aided by high score leaderboards)
- Showing off skills, such as by getting achievements to show on online profile
- Sharing one's gameplay with other people, such as by posting gameplay videos
- Showing off personal style, such as by wearing rare clothing items or collectibles
- Sharing own creative work, such as custom-made items, themes, or skins
- Spectating as a pastime, watching someone else compete or just play

Social metagame often arises spontaneously when players play together and talk about their play experience, but it can also be supported by the designer by the addition of game mechanics or online tools such as:

- Achievements that show off one's progress
- High scores and leaderboards that make it easy to rank oneself against others
- Leagues or clans in multiplayer games where players can self-organize into teams
- Streaming mode that lets players share their play sessions and allows others to spectate
- Content creation website where player can share items they created in the game
- Gamer profiles that tie all of these together and make it easy to find someone's contributions, relative rank, and so on

This kind of metagame is very common, and examples like participating in athletic competitions or making friendships over sports have been known since times immemorial. When translated into the world of computer or physical games, these might turn into participating in esports competitions or spectating by watching and sharing YouTube or Twitch videos. But regardless of the medium, this metagame lets us socialize with others who share the same passions.

### Game Modding

A different kind of a "game on top of the game" arises when the player decides not to be bound by the existing rules or implementation. They may write their own house rules for an existing card game. They may decide to use cheat codes or edit save files or AI scripts to change the rules of a computer game. They could also use the various third-party cheating tools to modify the contents of a game's memory at runtime to change outcomes in the game or to access locked content.

This kind of metagame is common in the computer game ecosystem and often treated as a fun way for players to "play with the game" in addition to playing the game. Game cheat codes and "trainers" (programs that modify a game's behavior) are common in the PC world.[19] Some developers go as far as publishing guides on how to modify the game, sometimes even distributing tools to make it easier, and entire communities spring up around sharing *mods* for the game.

At the same time, this kind of tinkering can be extremely undesirable in multiplayer games, in which it can be used for cheating, griefing (annoying other players), and other destructive multiplayer behaviors. Especially in competitive games and esports, modding can be seen as detrimental (with some exceptions for playing with mods that players agreed on beforehand). Console platforms like PlayStation or Xbox typically do not support game modifications, and competitive PC games sometimes resort to technical tools to detect trainers, network proxies, and other such tools that can be used for cheating.

---

19. Even so, development studios vary greatly in how they approach this kind of metagame. For example, the developers of *The Witcher 3* do not officially support any cheat codes, while the developers of *The Sims 4* made sure cheat codes are plentiful and even listed them right on the official website.

However, playing around with game rules is an old way for players to experiment with games, going back to the card players using "house rules" instead of official ones, or to players on 8-bit home computers using "POKE" commands to modify a game's memory addresses after loading. In contemporary design, supporting this kind of modding can be very positive for the developer by making the game more interesting for players, assuming the game's design supports that.

### Benefits of Metagame

Metagame can be doubly beneficial. On the design side, it can improve player experience, and on the business side, it can keep players excited about the game and keep bringing them back to the game day after day. The latter is important because an active player also helps grow the game. They will keep telling their friends about it, and they may be interested in buying expansion packs and other extras.

This is one reason why metagame is commonly encouraged, not just in games but also on platforms themselves. Consoles of the Xbox 360 and Play-Station 3 generation introduced achievements and leaderboards, which were also adopted by mobile platforms like Google Play and Apple iTunes. More recently, consoles of the Xbox One and PlayStation 4 generation introduced new and easy ways to record gameplay and broadcast it, or to spectate in competitive games played by others, supported by live broadcasting platforms like Twitch and YouTube. All of these add a social metagame that can be collaborative and creative as easily as competitive. Finally, PC platforms like Valve's Steam support mods explicitly by providing a platform and technical support for games to enable easy modding. All these are intended to keep bringing players back to the games—and to the platforms.

### Summary

In the previous chapter we looked at gameplay loops and the dynamic structure that emerges when players interact with systems and with each other over an extended period of time. In this chapter we zoom out even further and look at the interesting long-term macrostructure of this kind of gameplay. The key takeaways are:

- Games typically present the player with some kind of *fiction*. In some games this is a very specific *story*, but in other games it could be a general *fantasy*. The more story-oriented the game, the more it restricts the player's *agency* (the ability to affect the future) in order to give the designer more complete control over how the story will unfold.

- At the most basic level, stories can be understood in terms of the classic *three-act model*, which can be used to describe the large-scale *story arc* or smaller *episodic structures* of individual substories or levels.

- In story-oriented games, some of the typical narrative patterns include linear and branching stories, branch-and-merge and hub-and-spokes patterns, as well as larger compositions that can be built from these or other similar patterns. We paid special attention to open world games, which bring together a number of these narrative patterns, usually encoded in the form of quests. These provide good support for authorial control over the story and also maximize player autonomy and agency.

- Story-based games are especially aware of the importance of *pacing* and how adding variety and downtime can improve player experience. Non-story games also benefit from good pacing, but it is much harder to control when the player has more agency.

- Beyond the structure of a single game session, we can examine the *metagame* or how players keep interacting with the game and with each other even when they are not actively playing a session. We discuss two specific families: *mastery* metagame, focused on getting better at the game during future sessions, and *social* metagame, focused on getting recognition for one's actions in the game or simply even enjoying the game in the company of others. We also briefly discuss *modding* and creatively playing with the game's rules and implementation.

In the next and final chapter, we turn our attention to the prototyping process that designers use to turn this variety of tools and techniques into playable games.

### Further Reading

In this chapter we analyzed storytelling in terms of structural properties, but other approaches are also interesting and yield a variety of insights. Some further resources that might be useful:

- *Interactive Stories and Video Game Art* (Solarski, 2017a) discusses storytelling from a compositional perspective—how designers can compose visuals, space, and movement to shape the player's perception of their environment and the ongoing story. The book's numerous examples, sourced from television, film, and other media as well as games, will be useful to any student of design.

- *Video Game Storytelling* (Skolnick 2014) discusses stories and content arcs from a writer's perspective, focusing on how to craft a high-quality narrative. For more general narrative craftsmanship, screenwriting references can also be useful, such as *Story* (McKee 1997).

- *A Game Design Vocabulary* (Anthropy and Clark 2014) discusses stories from the perspective of player's response to choice and how players interpret those choices (or the lack thereof) and their consequences.

- Finally, on the interplay of content arcs and gameplay loops, Daniel Cook's "Loops and Arcs" essay (Cook 2012) is a worthwhile reference. On the topic of pacing from a designer's perspective, "Examining Game Pace" (Davies 2009) is a good study using *Call of Duty 4* as a guiding example.

## Individual Exercises

### 6.1. Game Fiction

Identify a game with a strong story as well as a game with a strong fiction, but without an emphasis on story. Compare them:

a. How does a strong story benefit the first game?

b. How does a strong fiction benefit the second game?

c. Can you imagine the first game without a story—just a fiction? How about the second game with a strong story? Would that work, and how might those games play?

### 6.2. The Three-Act Model

Pick a computer game you know well.

a. Describe the intensity arc from early to late game.

b. Does playing it fit into a three-act model, either as a game with an explicit content arc or a non-story game with early, mid, and late game sections? Describe how it does or in what ways it does not.

c. Does it split into smaller elements, such as levels or stages, that have their own arcs with their own ups and downs? Describe how it does or does not.

### 6.3. Narrative Patterns

Pick a computer game you know well. Find and describe some examples of narrative patterns present in this game—for example, in quests or missions.

### 6.4. Metagame

Pick a game you know well whose metagame you especially enjoy.

a. Describe in detail what it is about the metagame that you find enjoyable.

b. Identify whether the metagame is based on mastery, social elements, something different still, or a perhaps combination of the above.

c. Suggest one way in which this metagame could be improved further.

## Group Exercises

### G6.1. Board Games and the Three-Act Model

In this exercise we will practice analyzing the board game *Settlers of Catan* in the context of game stages and the three-act model. (This exercise assumes you have access to this particular board game. The instructor may suggest substituting a different game in its place.)

Play the game *Settlers of Catan* as a group and make a video or audio recording of the play session for transcription purposes below (low quality smartphone recording is just fine for this purpose). Go back through the recording and identify the rough timestamps when the following three stages of the game start and end.

- *Early game*, when players are mostly exploring and expanding on their own, with some trading.
- *Mid game*, when players are bumping into each other and competing and conflicts start to emerge over resources or placement of roads, settlements, and cities.
- *Late game*, when players are mostly focused on chasing the victory condition (trying to be the first to get to ten points).

These stages will *not* have clear boundaries, so do your best to identify when the game feels like it is definitely in early/mid/late game, and when it feels like it is in transition.

To complete the assignment, describe the following in detail for each stage of gameplay separately:

a. Describe when it started and ended and how long the game remained in that stage (in minutes).

b. Describe your subjective player experiences of being in that stage. What kinds of gameplay activities did you engage in? Use verbs like "competing," "socializing," "exploring," "educating," and other such words as appropriate.

c. Now consider the total game session. Did you have an experience of going through a three-act structure with rising intensity?

d. Identify how the actions that players performed changed over time and how this change contributed to this changing intensity.

# 7   Prototyping and Playtesting

We have explored a large variety of design elements in the last few chapters, from mechanics, systems, and dynamic aspects of gameplay to how players experience gameplay in the context of their own motivations. Now we can come back to the question posed all the way back in the first chapter—how do we put all these elements of design together to make a game?

In this chapter we present the process of building a game through iterative prototyping and playtesting. Designers rarely approach a new game by creating an entire design on paper and then implementing it all at once. That would be difficult because games are dynamic systems and as such they like to surprise their creators. They are composed of loops and feedback, and it is often hard to predict how exactly those will interact with each other once we put them in front of actual players.

Instead, designers tend to approach through exploration and iteration. We explore a bit of design at a time, implement it, test it, evaluate the results, and then feed what we learned back into evolving the design further and repeating the loop. Those implementations help guide the evolving design and help confirm or invalidate design decisions. We call this *prototyping*—continually building prototypes of the design and then incorporating the results into our vision of the game. This process is iterative as well as incremental, as prototypes evolve from small and fragmentary to larger and more complete structures that touch on larger and larger parts of the design.

In this chapter, we will examine:

- The development stages of a commercial game and how it turns from initial ideas—through a prototype—into a product
- How to develop an initial kernel of an idea into a concrete concept that is ready for prototyping

- How to iteratively grow the game's design by building prototypes and validating them through playtesting

Finally, we will end by examining how commercial studios proceed from this point to full commercial release, why it might be beneficial for student project groups to not do that, and what they should do instead.

**Motivating Example: *Project Highrise***

Throughout this chapter we will use the game *Project Highrise* to illustrate various steps of this production process.

*Project Highrise* is a business management game in which the player takes on the role of the architect, builder, and manager of various skyscrapers. Their job is to design and construct buildings, manage tenants, and—most importantly—make sure that everyone is happy and pays rent so that the player does not go bankrupt in the process. However, different types of tenants will have drastically different needs and expectations and they will affect each other's satisfaction in unexpected ways, and it is the player's job to resolve all conflicts and make the entire building ecosystem run smoothly and profitably.

**Figure 7.1**
Screenshot from *Project Highrise*

Although perhaps not as well known as some of the other games we examined previously, using *Project Highrise* in this chapter has a few specific benefits. First, it is one of the games we built at SomaSim, a studio I cofounded with Matthew Viglione. By using our own game as an example, I can speak directly to the details of our development process. Second, our project teams are quite small by industry standards, similar in size to student groups, and so these examples might be more relevant to student teams and independent teams of similar size.

## Production Stages

The process for turning an idea into a shipping game is not standardized and varies *greatly* depending on company size, budget, team size, or even the type of a game. But even across the different team sizes the development process can be seen as composed of several stages:

- *Concept.* In the beginning, we need to figure out the high-level *concept* of the game. What is the team making exactly, and who are we making it for? At this stage we figure out what the game is going to be, who the players are, what they would like about this game, and so on.
- *Prototyping and preproduction.* Once the concept is settled, we start to figure out the detailed design. This requires creating a more detailed plan of gameplay and the systems and mechanics that will bring it about and building pieces of the game to validate these design ideas in real life. We can accomplish this by building small *prototypes* of individual parts of the game that are often self-contained and throwaway, and we can also build a larger *first playable* that combines multiple systems and demonstrates how they all work together. The goal of this *preproduction* stage is to come up with a design that we are confident in and that is detailed enough that we can make a production schedule and budget.
- *Production.* Once the design, schedule, and budget are roughly known, we can go broad and build out all the levels, characters, quests, and everything else that the game needs. Production goes through its own substages, multiple alpha and beta milestones, culminating in an official release when the game is finally shipped to players.
- *Release and postrelease.* Releasing the game is a major milestone, but work does not end there. The team enters *maintenance* stage after the game

ships, releasing patches and bug fixes, rebalancing the game in response to player feedback, creating additional downloadable content, and so on. However, the recent trends of releasing games as an ongoing service or releasing early versions of the game under *early access* or *open beta* labels and continuing to improve it while it is already being sold to customers, makes it even harder to draw a firm line between the production, release, and postrelease phases.

All of these stages are important in commercial development, and the type of work changes over time. Most of the heavy design work happens at the earliest stages when all the options are wide open and a lot of work is needed to narrow it all down to a concrete design. Prototyping and preproduction help with that, and the goal of preproduction is to remove unknowns so that by the time the team enters production, they can focus on the hard work of building everything and not have to answer fundamental design questions.

Consequently, in the following sections we will focus on the initial stages, concepting and prototyping and preproduction, since they are central to how a game gets designed and developed. The later stages though important carry less design work, and we will review them very briefly. Finally, at the end of the chapter we will look specifically at how prototyping and preproduction can be adopted for student projects and classroom use.

## Game Concept

The very first stage of the game development process involves developing the game concept. Every game starts with some high-level vision, some initial kernel of an idea, but this is only a starting point. Before we can jump into mechanics and systems, we need to have a pretty good idea of what *exactly* we are going to be designing.

As so the first step is to flesh out this concept in more details so that we can understand what needs to be done. This concept stage typically serves several related purposes.

- *Understanding and specifying* the idea in enough detail that we understand the vision and understand what needs to be designed and built
- *Validating* the idea as commercially viable, such as by figuring out who the players are, how big of a market it is, how many copies might be sold, and so on

- *Communicating* the idea to other people outside of the team, especially for the purpose of pitching to get funding

**Understanding the Game Idea**

In the first stage of development, the team needs to come together on the vision of what game they are making. Sometimes this is very easy. The team has a clear idea of what exactly to build. At other times, different team members might have different ideas or goals, different understanding of the vision, and there is work required in bringing everybody together.

At this stage, the designer concentrates on figuring out the player experience and the general idea of gameplay. As discussed back in chapter 2, "Player Experience," the designer needs to consider player motivations of different player types and try to determine who is the player, what do they do in the game, and why.

We can start by asking ourselves questions about the game, such as the following:

- *What is the game fiction?* Explain who the player is playing as, what their role is in the game world, how they got there.
- *What is the gameplay?* Explain what the player is doing in the game world and what their activities are, both short-term and long-term.
- *Who are our players?* Explain the player's motivation, not as a character in the game but as the human playing the game—what player motivations it fulfills.

For example, on *Project Highrise*, we described our concept as follows:

- *Fiction*. The player is the architect, builder, and manager of skyscraper buildings. They create the designs and build them, move in tenants, manage them, and keep the entire building happy and profitable.
- *Gameplay*. On the smaller time scale, the fast loops involve building out floor space, finding and moving in tenants, and then collecting rent and using it to grow or improve the building, add on new floors, provide services, run utilities, fix problems, and so on as needed. The larger scale loops involve keeping the economy balanced while doing things to attract more and more prestigious tenants who will pay more in rent. This, in turn, requires saving up money to make expensive, large-scale improvements in order to make the building into a highly prestigious and sought-after property.

- *Player types.* The player's goal is to build and manage complex skyscraper ecosystems. This appeals to a combination of motivations—the strategic and tactical challenge of keeping a chaotic economy running and profitable as is common in management games, the exploratory aspect of being able to experiment with an ecosystem and seeing how it behaves, and the creative self-expression of being able to build and decorate a skyscraper building that reflects the player's style and aesthetic vision. We knew we were making a game that satisfies a mix of player motivations along the strategy, challenge, exploration, and design axes.

Note that we already make some references to specific details here. We note the genre (economy management), and we note some systems and mechanics (construction, money loops, expansions, prestige). This is okay. The description does not have to be purely abstract—just enough so that we do not get bogged down in details just yet. The goal is to create a description that is specific enough for everybody on the team to understand what the game is, but it is not a detailed design.

### Understanding the Market

If the game is intended to be sold commercially (as opposed to student projects or noncommercial pieces), it is crucial to also try to predict how the game might do in the market—how well it might sell, how many copies, at what prices, and so on. This is a difficult task, and precise predictions are impossible. Games are aesthetic products, and player reaction can vary wildly depending on how exactly the game plays and looks once it is finished.

But at this stage we can make some rough plans to at least make sure we are not starting down the wrong path, such as by trying to answer these questions.

- *What is the market for this game?* If we are making a management game as opposed to something geared toward a mass market, like an action game, how many players might be interested in this? Is this a niche game with limited appeal, or does it have broad appeal?
- *What is our competition, and how big is it?* It might be very hard for a newcomer to break in and get new players interested if there are already many games of this type (such as action platformers), if the platform is saturated (such as mobile app stores), or if most players are already locked in to a single game of the same type (such as *World of Warcraft* among massively multiplayer fantasy RPGs).

- *How will this game stand out, given the competition?* There needs to be something that sets this game apart from others, and it needs to be relevant to the target audience. This could be gameplay, or aesthetics, fiction, or something else entirely, but it needs to speak to the players we are trying to attract.

- *How big is the addressable audience?* If we are making a game for the Windows operating system, there are many more players on that platform than if we were making a game for MacOS or Linux. Similar observations apply to massively popular consoles like PlayStation or Xbox, contrasted with platforms with far fewer players. The size of the platform and its potential for growth needs to be central in this calculation.

- *What kinds of sales and unit pricing can we expect?* We should seek out relevant *comps* (that is, comparable products, such as games with similar gameplay and similar production values) and see if we can figure out how well they sold and at what price to get some idea of how well our game might sell if everything goes well.

We did all of these when concepting *Project Highrise*, for example:

- We compiled lists of other games related to our concept (similar genres or styles) and sought out information about how those games did in the market. The availability of different stats changes over time. For example, at that point, the SteamSpy website provided rather accurate player counts for computer games released on the Steam platform.

- We used market comparisons to validate our choice of platform (PC and Mac computer games) and to determine if it seemed possible to sell enough copies to justify the cost. Finally, market comps were crucial in figuring out pricing that would be on par with other games of its style and quality bar.

- We pursued multiple ideas to set the game apart. We focused on a genre that was underserved at that time; we chose a highly distinctive visual style with an immediately recognizable mid-twentieth-century flair; and we set up the theme and topic of the game to be recognizable to players of previous PC management games.

These are just some ideas to keep in mind during the concept phase. There are many more different things we could do to try to predict how well it might do in the market, and Futter (2017) describes market research in much more detail. But we will never get precise answers. The goal is not so much to predict winners, which is impossible, but rather to prevent obvious failures.

### Forming a Game Pitch

After doing the work of solidifying and validating the concept, it is often useful to condense the results into a quick *pitch document* that describes the game quickly and succinctly.

A pitch doc is most often used to get funding. This would be a document presented to potential publishers or funders to get them interested in the game concept. As such, pitch docs tend to be written in a very succinct way, such that they can be understood quickly. Also, since the intended audience are people outside of the team (such as potential funders), it is common to use other games as points of reference so that they can quickly grasp how this concept compares and contrasts with what is already on the market.

Pitch documents are not standardized, and every publisher or funder will have their own expectations about what they would like to see. However, some common elements of the pitch doc include:

- *An elevator pitch*—a quick, pithy, ten-second blurb about what the game is and what is interesting about it. These can take a long time to get right, but they are very useful in getting the essence of the concept across to the audience

- *A design summary*—perhaps a paragraph or a few paragraphs summarizing the fantasy or the story of the game and providing an overview of what it would be like to play it

  Some teams like to further condense the design summary into *design pillars*—a few unique and central elements of the game without which the design would not "stand." For example, design pillars for *Minecraft* might include random world generation, mining and crafting, building fantastic creations, and playing with friends on the same map. These help the reader compare the game to what they already know and help communicate where the central core of the game lies.

- *Market comparison*—for commercial games, these would be the results of analyzing the market, such as description of target platforms, audience size, pricing ideas, and so on. Comparisons with other games, including ratings such as Steam reviews or Metacritic scores, are also useful.

Funding pitches will typically also include appropriate business data, such as team size, expected cost of development, and so on. These are not germane to our discussion here. See the "Further Reading" section for additional resources on the structure and format of pitch documents.

In addition to external communication, a pitch doc can also be very useful internally to communicate the vision within the team and keep everybody in sync. During a game's development, many new ideas will keep appearing across the team, so a succinct design concept can help remind everybody what they are making and why, and help decide which new ideas should be incorporated and which can be discarded.

## From Concept to Prototyping: Kelly Guidelines

How do we know when our concept is clear enough to start building out the design? Different teams have different traditions on how to answer to this question. However, Tadhg Kelly's "Seven Deadly Questions" (Kelly 2014) is a set of particularly useful guidelines for determining this and can be used with a variety of team sizes and game types. These heuristics are focused on keeping the prototyping and development process sharp and focused, but without requiring a lot of upfront documentation.

In his work as a design consultant, Kelly noticed that it was easy for teams to get distracted during development and lose sight of the original vision for two reasons: first, because game design is hard to communicate succinctly, so the vision gets blurred over time, and second, because development and playtesting invariably produces a stream of new ideas which can be exciting but also distracting. Teams that get distracted and lose focus of their original vision will have a much more difficult time coming up with a coherent game in the end.

To prevent this situation, he suggests a set of seven questions to be answered by the team before they transition away from the concept phase. These questions are meant to be used instead of a full, formal design document. The answers are easier to produce and still allow for a lot of flexibility, but they document the core of the vision and become a set of shared foundations to help remind everybody what game they are making. These answers can then be used to filter and cull any ideas that come up during prototyping and development. Any additional idea can be checked against these foundations, and if it does not reinforce the shared vision, perhaps it is best to drop it on the discard pile.

Kelly's seven questions are as follows.[20]

1. *What is the urgency in the game?* In other words, what is the struggle or the challenge that the player confronts in the game in terms of gameplay as well as in terms of the fiction? A game needs to have some urgency, something gripping the player's attention and imagination to keep the player interested.

   In a game like *Tetris*, the urgency comes from blocks falling from the sky relentlessly and faster than the player can deal with them. In *Minecraft*, the world is dangerous, and the player must build everything by hand and fend for themselves. Meanwhile a game like *The Sims* might present the familiar struggle of living as an adult who has a difficulty making ends meet.

2. *What is the player's job?* Again, not the player's character's job in the story, not the narrative job. Rather, how can we succinctly describe what the player does when they play the game, for example, in one word or a short phrase?

   In *Tetris*, the player's job is "sorter of puzzle pieces." In *Tomb Raider*, they are an "adventurer." And in *Rome: Total War*, they are a "general." The major benefit of establishing a clear job early is that it guides the player's and the designer's understanding of what the player will be asked to do. The player in *Rome: Total War* understands they will be commanding armies and probably will not be asked to micromanage individual soldiers and keep them happy.

   Job description also helps the designer recognize and halt the temptation to overload the player with too many jobs. Sometimes it becomes very tempting to pile additional jobs and types of activity on the player as the design evolves, but games work better if the player has only one job or a very small cluster of related jobs.

3. *What are the player's inputs?* Do they use a controller, or a mouse and keyboard combination, or maybe a touch screen? And how will in-game actions be assigned to the buttons, joysticks, touch screen areas, and so on?

---

20. These questions have been reinterpreted using the vocabulary we have been developing so far in the text, because the original text uses terms like "verbs" and "actions" in a slightly different sense. Special thanks to Kelly for additional clarifications of these points over email.

The choice of inputs will greatly influence how well the player can accomplish various goals. Different inputs have different affordances. For example, a touch screen makes it very easy to pick and move items on the game screen, which is much harder with a controller, but a controller enables very complex character navigation through virtual space. Also, when dealing with a controller, having to remember the various actions and how they map to only a few buttons will be taxing to the player, and the game needs to account for good input mappings and training the player to use them.

4. *Are player activities extensible?* This touches on core mechanics. What are they, and do they change over time? Can they be upgraded or modified or combined with each other to produce more complex behaviors?

   For example, in a war game the basic actions involve moving troops, attacking, or defending—but if units can be upgraded or their stats can unlock new types of attacking or defending, it will lead to desirably complex gameplay. Or in fighting game, different kinds of attacks may combine with each other into *combos* with new and interesting characteristics. Activities that can be modified and extended are better than ones that remain static over the duration of the game.

5. *Are there three (or more) resource types?* Kelly points out that even a simple sport like *tennis* already has four resource types—a tennis racket that is an equippable item with its own characteristics, a tennis ball that is a token that gets exchanged between players, stats such as points or sets, and territory control in the sense that the player's position on the court has huge strategic importance.

   Some other examples of resource type triplets from common games include "guns, bullets, health" from *Quake* or "land, spells, life points" in *Magic the Gathering*. It is important for games to have not just a variety of one type of resources, but also a variety of resource types, or, for games that do not focus on resource management, a variety of types of mechanics. Having more types with various tradeoffs will feel more interesting to the player than just adding more elements within a single type.

6. *Is there a defining rule?* Although games have a variety of rules and mechanics, many successful games have one or more defining rules which are unique to this game or the genre and without which the game just would not be what it is.

These are often unique constraints or tradeoffs. In *chess*, the defining rule is the check rule and the resulting vulnerability of the king. In a game like *FarmVille*, it is appointment-based mechanics, planting something and then having to come back at a specified time to collect it. In a game like *Ico*, it is always having to protect the safety of the companion character who keeps following the player. If we removed these rules, the games would no longer be recognizably the same. Having this kind of a unique overarching concern, which cuts across all parts of gameplay, gives the player interesting new problems to overcome, and differentiates the game from the rest.

7. *What are you testing?* Games challenge the player in multiple ways, but there should be one or a few dominant gameplay challenges that are core to the game, and these challenges should be concrete and actionable. For example, *Tetris* tests the player's ability to sort shapes under time pressure, fighting games like *Tekken* test the ability to execute complex moves and attacks with perfect timing, and city builders like *SimCity* test the ability to manage resources and space allocation. The player should be able to understand what is being asked of them and get feedback on how they are doing to avoid confusion and frustration about what they are supposed to do in the game.

Answering questions like these will help the team crystallize their vision for the game and get it ready for implementation. It will also help filter and prioritize new ideas as they inevitably come in during prototyping.

### Prototyping

Once the concept is sufficiently clear, it is time to work out the design in detail. This is when we go from a high-level vision to detailed specifications of gameplay and the systems and mechanics that will bring them about.

We call this stage "preproduction," because it happens before full production of the title. The goal of preproduction is to figure out the detailed design, experiment with the vision, and resolve the various unknowns so that we can enter production with a clear idea of what needs to be built, how much time it will take, and how many people.

As we mentioned before, it is uncommon for the development team to come up with the full design first and then implement it all at once and expect it to work. We are building dynamic systems, and their behavior is difficult to anticipate. Some surprises are internal. The interactions between systems can be chaotic and unpredictable, especially if they are composed of feedback loops that feed into each other. But by far the biggest source of surprise are players. They are curious, smart, driven, and generally always end up taking actions that the designer failed to predict.

Instead of an upfront design, we do the design and implementation as an interleaved, iterative process. We explore a bit of design at a time, implement it, test and evaluate the results, and then feed what we learned back into evolving the design further and repeating the loop.

## Playable Prototypes

There are two basic approaches to testing design ideas: building small *individual prototypes* of different parts of the game or building an *accumulative prototype* that integrates many design elements together. Teams can also use both approaches together as needed.

Individual prototypes are fast implementations of specific design ideas intended to test specific things in separation. A good example might be a prototype of a combat system in an action fighting game or the prototype of different crafting systems in a role-playing game. They test whether that particular system or set of mechanics is enjoyable, independent of everything else.

These kinds of prototypes usually answer only some specific questions, and they are not intended to last or to be incorporated into the final product. For this reason, a common practice is to implement them as *throwaways*—build them quickly without any attention to good engineering practices and reusing as much existing code and assets as possible (such as using temporary visual assets, code from previous projects, and so on). The only thing that matters is proving or disproving some specific theories about parts of the design, then discarding the prototype and moving on.

A different approach is to build an accumulative prototype, which consists of a number of different parts of the game and tests how the game plays when they are all working together. This approach is more common in systems-heavy games like war games or management games, since those are very sensitive to the quality of integration of different systems and not just the quality of the constituent pieces. This is also how we approached the development on *Project Highrise*, which is a very systems-heavy kind of a game.

Because of the sheer scale of an accumulative prototype and the amount of work that goes into it, it is more common for teams to not build them as throwaways but rather build them as small playable demos which can, over time, turn into the actual game. The reason for this is both economic and technical. Having put a lot of time into an accumulative prototype, the team might be reluctant to scrap all this work and take the extra time to rebuild everything from scratch. Also, software engineering folklore suggests that fixing up bad but functional software results in a higher quality product than attempting to rewrite it from scratch (Spolsky 2000).

If the team decides on an accumulative prototype, they can still use temporary art assets that will be later replaced, but they should implement the technical aspects with an eye towards the future (follow good engineering practices and build it in an extensible and expandable way, to minimize the need to fix it up later). The result of this kind of a prototype might be a *playable demo* of a game that shows how the game would play but does not have the breadth of content or game-specific art assets.

In either case, it can be very beneficial to resist using polished visual assets during this stage to allow for high iteration speed. For example, in level-based games, it is common practice to start by *whiteboxing* level layout, that is, creating the desired layout using simple untextured boxes instead of final-looking assets to make it easier to change and iterate quickly until the desired spatial design is achieved (Solarski 2017a, 7).

Regardless of which prototyping approach the team takes or a combination of the two, the process will be similar—we test out different design ideas and see how they play out when integrated with each other and put in front of the player.

**Iterative Process**

With the concept worked out, we can start on a cycle of producing prototypes and evaluating them. A typical sequence of steps may look as follows, and the process is very easy to customize.

- *Conceptual design.* In the first step, we focus on some elements of the game, do a more detailed design, and plan out what to build. We could be adding some new systems or changing existing elements based on what we have observed so far, and so on. At this step we figure out some partial design and try to work out all the details we can.

**Analog and digital prototypes.** In order to prototype quickly, it is sometimes tempting to move away from digital prototypes, implemented on the computer, and turn towards *analog* or *paper prototypes*, implemented using physical game pieces like cards, game boards, tokens, and play money. Paper prototypes can be much faster to implement than digital ones. It is much easier to print out and cut up paper cards or draw a game board on a piece of cardboard than to implement a similar setup using any game engine. Analog prototypes are popular in classroom settings because of this speed and because they are much easier for novice developers to work with.

However, analog prototypes are not commonly used in the video game industry. Their main drawback is that they are great for prototyping games that have similar mechanics to card or board games but not good for other types, such as games that rely on physical performance or implicit mechanics. Imagine, for example, doing a paper prototype of an arcade fighting game. This prototype would not help us answer any questions about game feel, attack timing, choice of input button or combos, and so on. For another example, a game like *SimCity* relies very much on implicit mechanics that the player learns over time and a complex simulation of the world state. Attempting to replicate this kind of a simulation with paper and human players would fail to scale.

But for digital games that already resemble analog games, paper prototyping can be a very good fit. Collectible card games like *Hearthstone* or *Gwent* can be particularly good for prototyping using paper cards played with friends, as are tactics games and war games with sufficiently self-contained, explicit mechanics. (Brathwaite and Schreiber 2009) is a great resource for learning more about analog prototyping.

- *Implement the design.* We build a playable version of our new design element. This can mean adding to the existing prototype so that with each iteration the prototype grows more complex and closer to a game demo. However, some tests may be easier to evaluate by building separate standalone throwaway prototypes.
- *Playtest the implementation.* We set a goal based on what we want to test. For example, does our new system work as intended? Is it enjoyable for players? Do players understand what it is and how to interact with it? The real test happens when we put this in front of players, have them interact with the newly implemented elements, and see what happens.
- *Evaluate the playtest.* Examine the results with a critical eye, whether the design and implementation succeeded in the goals we set for ourselves

for this iteration and also how they support the overall goals for the game.

- *Modify the design.* See how the results affect the design going forward and how it affects other elements that have already been designed and implemented.

Then go back to the first step and repeat this all over again!

This prototyping is deliberately very iterative. With each cycle, we repeat the same steps—we plan, build, play, evaluate, and then make decisions about what to do.

This process is also very similar to prototyping in other disciplines, such as industrial or software design (Brooks 2010). In software development this has been well described by a model called the *Boehm spiral* (Boehm 2000) among others. Figure 7.2 illustrates how this spiral might look when adapted to game prototyping.

The spiral starts with designing some aspect of the game, which we implement and playtest. If the test was successful, we can keep this element

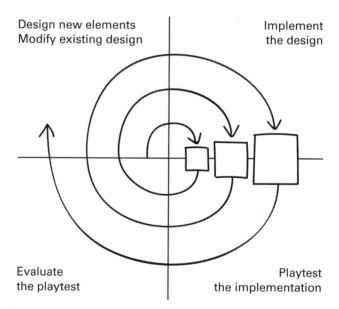

**Figure 7.2**

A game prototyping spiral diagram, modeled after the Boehm spiral, with the game prototype growing and improving with each iteration

and integrate it into the game thus far, perhaps with additional ideas for how to improve it further. And then we design another aspect, implement, playtest, and so on. In this way, we grow the game with each successive playtest—and quite likely, we also grow our prototype towards a high quality "first playable" build.

Even though this kind of a spiral process has become common in software development, it is a relatively recent development. It succeeds an older development model that involved building different pieces of software in separation, in "silos" disconnected from each other (for example, into different functional modules), and then integrating them together in the end. However, this approach was infamous for painful and drawn-out integration phases, during which many incompatibilities, assumptions, and defects surfaced and had to be resolved. With the benefit of hindsight, we now know that it is difficult to create module specifications so detailed that we can predict exactly how they will work together once assembled.

In comparison, the iterative approach puts integration first. The different parts of the product get built out together, instead of in separation. The main significant benefit of this process is gradual reduction of risk and increase of confidence in the design. Each time we go through the cycle, we both try out new additions but also reconfirm that what we already designed works well together. And if we discover it does not, we can observe that in the playtest and fix it.

## Playtesting

Early in development, designers and developers test their own game by playing it, which is very easy because they do not need to be taught how to play (this is especially important very early on when the user interface and controls are still a work in progress and the game is undecipherable to outsiders). Later during the development process, the team might extend an invitation to their friends and family, or perhaps other developers on other teams, to play the game and give feedback. Finally, during late production, the team may wish to bring in external testers who have never played the game to see how the experience looks through the eyes for the first-time user.

Running a successful playtest means trying to see the game through another player's eyes. This requires being a dispassionate observer of one's own game and the player's reaction to it. Developers may find this stage to be quite unpleasant because it can be difficult for impassioned creators to put an unfinished game before an audience and have to see their reaction to known problems. But it is an important part of the process because watching player reaction will also help us uncover *unknown* problems.

Some heuristics for running a playtest:

- When playtesting, we need to let players play and make mistakes without correcting them or telling them what to do. This can be difficult, as players inevitably make mistakes and get confused, but learning is always part of gameplay. As tempting as it is, we should try not to correct them but rather observe what they do. Only in exceptional circumstances, when the player is truly stuck or if they encountered a bug in the game, it may be good to give them a little push, but it should be avoided.

- It is very useful to ask players to narrate what they are doing as they are doing it and to ask them to narrate how they feel as they play. This gives us an idea of what the game looks like through the player's eyes and what kind of an experience they are having. And if they get engrossed in the game, they will stop narrating, which is a great sign, but we may need to prompt them again every now and then.

- It is very useful to note down what they say, but we must not take it literally. Instead, we pay attention to what they do and how they feel and the emotional content of what they tell us. When a player says something like "this enemy is too hard," they are not asserting literally that the enemy difficulty is too high. Rather, it shows that the player is frustrated with not being able to defeat the enemy. But there could be a variety of solutions depending on context. For example, maybe we give the player a weapon buff or maybe have the player train a bit more and build up their skills before they face this enemy, and so on (also including not doing anything at all).

- Finally, we observe their failure modes as well as their successes. Are the players learning what they should be learning? Are they acting in expected ways, and are you meeting your playtest goals?

In order to ensure that players are fully engaged with the game, developers will routinely go to great lengths to make players comfortable and unselfconscious. Large development studios or outsourced playtesting companies may ask testers to play in especially equipped rooms where developers cannot interact with the player directly and can only watch their reactions through a webcam and screensharing setup. Smaller developers may instead opt for a more informal setting, like having strangers play at conventions or conferences, or perhaps letting them play at home with a specially instrumented build that sends back data about the tester's progress.

Each playtest session will routinely produce a huge list of notes, ranging from small items (such as little UI improvements, small bugs, and so on) to larger observations that could have larger knock-on effects on the game (such as observing that an entire system is just not working as intended).

This list is going to contain a variety of items, so the first step is to *triage* the notes based on importance. In other words, we sort them into three categories:

1. "To do" list, items that are obviously problematic or important improvements that need to happen. Most bugs fall into this category, as well as unambiguous lessons from the playtest. These should be fixed immediately.

2. "To consider" list, items that might be worth exploring, such as suggestions from players or ideas that the team came up with during the playtest. However, they may be unclear or might have knock-on effects that need to be explored further. These items will likely require additional work to figure out whether or what should be done in response.

3. "Won't do" list, one-off items that were noted during the playtest, but they do not need to be changed immediately, or they are not reproducible. Some examples might be players reacting negatively to temporary art assets that are on schedule to be replaced, or players not noticing some important bit of information and drawing incorrect conclusions about what happened. These items should be tracked but do not need to be acted on unless more than one player starts noticing them, in which case they might need additional consideration.

The reason for this triage is that not all suggestions are equally important, and different suggestions can involve different amounts of work or have different knock-on effects. After triaging, we can then prioritize these items and incorporate them into our work scheduling as needed.

But these decisions must not be made during playtest. When playtesting, we just take down all of the observations without filtering. It is only afterwards that we should go through the list and start categorizing and making decisions about how to feed the results into the next prototyping iteration.

## Documenting Design

As the concept and prototyping stages progress, the team creates a more thorough description of the design in sufficient detail that it could be shared with other team members for implementation.

This detailed shared vision often ends up in the form of a *design document*. The name is a bit of an anachronism, reflecting that in the past, one could see a single document which encyclopedically described various elements of the game. But contemporary studios are much more likely to store design documentation via project-specific wikis or online tools like Google Drive that can contain a wide variety of media files (not just text documents, but also concept art, screenshots, video clips, and so on) and can be quickly updated during design iteration.

On large teams, it is very important for this communication to be well documented and precise in order to make sure everyone is building the same thing and everyone is coordinated. On teams with tens or hundreds of members communication becomes difficult, and documentation helps ensure that all designers are working on the same shared vision of the game and that other disciplines (art, engineering, marketing, etc.) also understand exactly how the game is intended to play.

However, on smaller teams where direct communication is fast and easy, maintaining such a detailed specification might not be worth the time. For example, on *Project Highrise*, the team was small enough for everyone to talk to everyone else without much friction. So, we found the happy medium to be a shared collection of Google Docs that was used only initially to start the prototyping process with a shared vision. But once prototyping started in earnest, we stopped updating these docs and switched to using video chat, emails, and "to do" lists to communicate how the design was changing.

Though we do not go into further detail here, the "Further Reading" section contains pointers to more information about design documents, their structure, and their uses.

## Finishing Iteration

Following the iterative process, we go back and forth improving our design, implementing it, playtesting, and then drawing conclusions from the playtest to further improve our design. With each round through the spiral, our design and playable build grows more complete. So, when do we stop?

Fortunately or not, there is no clear answer to this. Very rarely do we get to stop when we are satisfied with the results, when we achieved the design we were aiming for and nothing more can be improved about it. But most of the time, the "best" design is always elusive. We can always explore one more design change or implement one more idea.

Most of the time, we stop when we have to—when we achieve a design we are sufficiently satisfied with but before we run out of time and resources. But this aspect of design iteration is not a negative. Constraints force us to focus on parts that are important to us and cut out extraneous details. As Leonard Bernstein was said to have quipped, "to achieve great things, two things are needed: a plan and not quite enough time." Constraints are always a part of the creative process.

## Production and Beyond

A student project may very well stop at this point—creating a complete design from the initial idea, through preproduction, to a "first playable" prototype. On the other hand, a commercial project will typically continue from preproduction to full production.

Preproduction ends once the team has learned enough about the game and the design to be able to make a confident production plan that lists what needs to be done, how many people and resources will be needed, and what kind of a timeline is expected.

If the plan is accepted, the team enters the *production* phase, and the focus turns towards building all the pieces and putting them together into the final product. This is also when the team usually grows to fit the needs of the production plan. This phase itself also has multiple substages.

Early in production, the goal is to create an *alpha* build, which is a playable demo that is *systems-complete* (includes all the various gameplay systems and loops). This is not a complete game, and it can use unfinished art assets or level design, but it should demonstrate how the systems and mechanics work together. At this stage, the game is still extremely raw. It may even be unstable and crash, but the team starts playing it regularly as well as sending it to trusted external testers to get playtesting and feedback. There are usually multiple alpha builds as the team progresses through gameplay implementation and adds more content.

Some studios also have a tradition of building a *vertical slice*. Just like the alpha build, it includes various gameplay systems and loops, but also a small fraction of content which is polished to shippable quality (for example, one level that includes one enemy type and only one special weapon, but having been implemented and iterated on so that they could be shipped in the final version). Vertical slices are helpful in showing how the finished game would play based on just a fraction of the content expected of the entire finished game. However, they are only useful in some genres of games, such as level-based games, where a lot of work goes into content production. In other genres, such as simulation and strategy games, vertical slices are not very useful because building out all systems to high quality is very close to actually finishing the game.

After finishing alpha, the next milestone is to complete remaining content production, integrate all of the playtesting feedback, and produce a sequence of *beta* builds that are not yet final but fairly representative of the final game and good enough to start playtesting with external testers. Beta usually means that the game is *content-complete*. Gameplay and content are all built out fully, although they do not have to be tuned or polished quite to shipping standards (maybe some assets are missing or unpolished, maybe the UI is not quite as easy to use as it could be, and so on). At this stage, a lot of playtesting happens, both by dedicated quality assurance teams as well as other developers (or maybe even dedicated players who were invited to participate), and it routinely unearths tons of problems to be fixed.

As all bugs get fixed, all problems addressed, and all rough edges polished off, the game enters final rounds of bug testing, focusing mainly on bona fide errors and crashes. Console games also need to pass platform quality certification at this stage. This produces a sequence of *release candidate* builds that get tested as if they were going to be shipped to customers. Once a release candidate passes all testing and becomes approved for release, it is called the *gold master*, or, less poetically, the *release to manufacturing* build.

Finally, after the game is released, the work is not over. Some ongoing work will be needed to support the game (fix bugs, add features and enhancements) or to produce additional content that will be released or sold to players. This is especially true in the case of "games as a service," or, in other words, games where players are expected to keep playing and purchasing various additional content over an extended period of time, in which case a production team might be needed indefinitely, as long as the game is live.

This separation of preproduction and production can seem rigid, and it often is because its main purpose is risk reduction. The goal is to try to control how much the game will cost, partly by trying to prevent late-stage changes being made to the game's design. The reason is that the later into development, the more expensive it is to implement sudden design changes, especially on large and interconnected teams in which each design element needs to be coordinated across multiple departments (design, art, engineering, writing, and so on). However, this rigidity also has a price. Game design often relies on experimentation and exploration to find a compelling design, and sometimes inspiration likes to strike late in the process when many pieces have been built and developers see how they work together. This tension between desire for flexibility and the costs of flexibility does not have a resolution and continues to haunt games during scheduling and production.

However, on smaller teams, this process can be drastically simplified. When the team is small, communication and interaction are much easier. For example, on *Project Highrise*, we transitioned very gradually from preproduction to production without going through a specific kick-off process. We did not build a detailed production plan, instead we created a rough schedule with a lot of built-in flexibility oriented around alpha, beta, and release milestones. Finally, although we did make some late-stage design changes, they were easy to absorb into our schedule because the team was small and dynamic.

In the end, a production schedule is a communication tool, used to make sure everybody is working in concert towards shared goals. Smaller teams, in which communication overhead is small and team members are generalists, can be much more flexible about how they approach their scheduling.

## Ideas for Student Prototyping

So far, we have discussed the commercial production process. We will now shift our attention to student projects and propose a few tweaks which might be worth considering. Student projects are not under pressure to produce commercially successful works, but they have other constraints as well as opportunities.

Please consider the following to be ideas and suggestions only. They are intended to improve team projects in a school setting, but since they might or might not fit the vision of particular courses or programs, please adopt and adapt them as desired.

## Shorter Production Cycle

A multistage production process is typical for a commercial studio, but in a classroom setting it might be too heavy. Specifically, student teams typically work under a much tighter time constraint. They have one quarter or one semester to make a game, maybe two or three in some cases, and limited amount of time to devote to coursework. They are also learning both design and development and will benefit from taking the time to experiment.

In my experience with teaching game development in a one-quarter or two-quarter setup, I tend to concentrate on concepting and preproduction and not focus on the production stage. In this setting, a typical schedule might look as follows:

- Short amount of time spent on concepting
- Initial milestone: produce a design vision and a pitch doc
- Large amount of time spent on iterative design and prototyping
- Final milestone: a playable demo that presents the cumulative design

It seems more beneficial for students on a tight schedule to spend time experimenting with design and prototyping and produce a playable demo even if it lacks broad content. However, for a large student project (such as a one-year "capstone" project), it might be beneficial to follow the commercial process more closely.

## Scaling Prototyping Scope

Although this text elaborates the process of making a new game design from start to finish, a full design process might not be appropriate for all types of projects. For example, beginner students may be more comfortable with starting with an existing game design and putting their own twist on it rather than starting a new design process from scratch.

The following are some ideas for different types of projects that could be adapted to different team experience levels and course requirements.

- A *reskin* or *clone* game is one that takes the mechanics of an existing game wholesale and creates a new implementation with new visuals. For example, a reskin of a classic game like *Pac-Man* would follow the original mechanics, perhaps with slight tweaks, and provide different level layout and different kinds of character sprites. Making a reskin can be an appropriate starting point for new programmers and new designers for whom just implementing a reskin by itself will be challenging enough.

- A *variant* game is one that takes mechanics of an existing game and puts some new twist on them and still remain in the same genre and style. For example, a variant of *Pac-Man* with some mechanics added, removed, or remixed with other games, and so on. This kind of design approach presents interesting design challenges but remains well constrained and suitable for single-course projects.

- A *genre* game would be one that adheres to conventions of a genre, such as expectations around systems and gameplay, but comes up with its own brand-new systems, setting, etc., by drawing on many inspirations. This is a more advanced design task than making a variant because the changes are on the level of systems and gameplay loops.

- An *experimental* game could try to develop brand new gameplay or player experience elements or combine existing genres in completely unexpected ways, and so on, for the purpose of creating something unprecedented. Similarly, a *genre-bending* game could take genre expectations and subvert them in some way, such as by removing crucial systems and building a game around whatever is left. These kinds of approaches can be very interesting but the results can be very unpredictable, as can be the amount of prototyping time required.

These are just some ideas for project. The main constraint is going to come from the requirements of the course and the goals of project teams and how much they can invest in the design process.

## Supporting Portfolio Development

Game projects are often useful for students as portfolio pieces when interviewing for jobs in game development or other disciplines. It might be beneficial for students to consider how to focus their project to make it an interesting showcase piece in the future.

For one, student projects do not have to worry about commercial success. This gives students a lot of freedom to try things that they might not be able to do if they worked on a commercial product. Experimenting with gameplay or technology that is interesting but not yet commercially viable (for example, alternative reality games) or focusing the game on showcasing some specific skills (for example, visual effects) can be a good way to make a portfolio piece stand out.

Secondly, students may want to consider sharing the game on a public independent game portal, such as *Itch.io*. These portals serve a double purpose as places to store and showcase projects as well as community sites where players and developers interact. This can be a good way to host a project for public viewing and also to get thoughts and feedback from a community of other people interested in game development.

Finally, submitting the game to student festivals is always an option worth considering. Festivals that accept student submissions, like *IndieCade* or the *Independent Games Festival*, are very competitive and getting accepted is prestigious. However, students should research those festivals thoroughly to get a feeling for the expected quality bar. Furthermore, different festivals have different house styles, and they might prefer particular genres or types of gameplay above others, which also needs to be researched and taken into consideration.

## Summary

In this chapter, we have examined the process that game development teams use to turn concepts and design ideas into shippable games.

- First, we examined the overall *stages of development* as typically experienced in game studios. We looked at the role of concepting, followed by preproduction and prototyping, then followed by production, release, and postrelease work.

- We looked at the details of the game *concept stage* and the various purposes it serves. A good concept can help the team understand and validate the design they have in mind and help validate the market feasibility of the idea. This game concept can also be turned into a pitch document, which can be used to communicate this idea to others, such as internally within the company or externally to funders or others.

- For small teams specifically we described the idea of a short list of questions that should be answered before declaring the concepting stage complete. Following Kelly (2014), these questions can be replacement for a detailed game design document at this early stage.

- After concepting, we turned our attention to the *preproduction stage* (specifically prototyping the game design ideas) and introduced the concept of individual and accumulative *prototypes*. We examined the iterative process through which design ideas get turned into prototypes that are playtested and used to improve the design. We also examined the *playtesting* process in more detail and how this back-and-forth between design, implementation, and testing leads to a high-quality result. Finally, we reviewed the transition away from prototyping and the role of *production* and postrelease stages in commercial development.

- We finished with some ideas for student projects and how they can benefit from skipping a full production stage in order to focus on other aspects that are specifically useful for students.

## Further Reading

On the topic of production stages, a number of great resources exist. The following books feature especially detailed descriptions of planning, prototyping, and playtesting:

- *Advanced Game Design* (Sellers 2017), chapters 11–12
- *Game Design Workshop* (Fullerton 2008), chapters 6–9
- *The Art of Game Design* (Schell 2008), chapters 23–25

On the topic of the games business in general, a very approachable introduction is the *GameDev Business Handbook* (Futter 2017). For games that follow the free-to-play or "games as a service" model specifically, *The Pyramid of Game Design* (Lovell 2018) covers the related business aspects in great detail. And since the field changes at a rapid pace, interested readers may also find value in following industry websites such as *Gamasutra* and *GamesIndustry.Biz*.

On the specific topic of game pitch docs and outside communication, some the aforementioned resources also have relevant information.

- *GameDev Business Handbook* (Futter 2017), chapter 6
- *Game Design Workshop* (Fullerton 2008), chapters 13–14
- *The Art of Game Design* (Schell 2008), chapters 27–29

Finally, for readers interested in the history of iterative design and development, specifically in the context of software, *The Mythical Man Month* (Brooks 1975) and *The Design of Design* (Brooks 2010) are great references with resources for further exploration.

## Group Exercises

*Note:* The following exercises are intended for students or teams starting on a new project.

### G7.1. Project Pitch

Prepare a one-page document that presents your project pitch. It should include the following components:

- A brief elevator pitch in the form of one or a few short, snappy sentences
- A design summary describing the gameplay in the course of several paragraphs
- A description of your design pillars
- Callouts for any games that served as inspiration for specific mechanics or systems

### G7.2. Game Design Heuristics

Answer all of Kelly's seven questions in relation to your game. Did answering these questions prompt you to adjust your design in any way? If so, how?

### G7.3. Iterative Development

Imagine your project in the context of the iterative development spiral—designing some aspects, implementing, playtesting, reviewing the results, integrating the results, and looping back. What are the first elements you would want to implement and playtest, and why? What are the next elements that build on those?

# Conclusion

And so, in the journey through this text, we have now examined a vast array of design elements, mechanics, systems, gameplay loops, and player experiences, and finally finished with this chapter, pointing out the way for how to put it all together.

So, where do we go from here?

Now, armed with these concepts, the next step is to practice them yourself. There is no better teacher of design than implementing our own designs and seeing how they actually work when we put them in front of players.

What awaits you next, is taking that terrifying, exhilarating next step, and building your own games.

Good luck!

# References

Abt, Clark C, et al. 1965. *Counter-Insurgency Game Design Feasibility and Evaluation Study*. Washington, DC: Advanced Research Projects Agency. https://archive.org/details/DTIC_AD0475846.

Adams, Ernest, and Joris Dormans. 2012. *Game Mechanics: Advanced Game Design*. Berkeley, CA: New Riders.

Adams, Harold W. 1970. "The Design Dilemma: Games for Whom?" *Proceedings of the 9th Symposium*. National Gaming Council. 136–143. https://archive.org/details/ERIC_ED049109.

Anthropy, Anna, and Naomi Clark. 2014. *A Game Design Vocabulary: Exploring the Foundational Principles Behind Good Game Design*. Upper Saddle River, NJ: Addison-Wesley.

Avalon Hill, Inc. 1971. "Avalon Hill Philosophy." *The General Magazine*, July–Aug: 2–3. https://archive.org/details/GeneralMagazineVol8i2.

Bartle, Richard. 1996. "Hearts, Clubs, Diamonds, Spades: Players Who Suit MUDs." Technical Report, Muse Ltd., Colchester. Accessed October 27, 2018. http://mud.co.uk/richard/hcds.htm.

Barwood, Hal, and Noah Falstein. n.d. *The 400 Project*. Accessed September 17, 2018. http://www.finitearts.com/Pages/400page.html.

Bjork, Staffan, and Jussi Holopainen. 2004. *Patterns in Game Design*. Needham, MA: Charles River Media.

Boehm, Barry. 2000. "Spiral Development: Experience, Principles, and Refinements." Report CMU/SEI-2000-SR-008, Software Engineering Institute, Carnegie Mellon, Pittsburgh. Accessed November 14, 2018. http://www.dtic.mil/dtic/tr/fulltext/u2/a382590.pdf.

Brathwaite, Brenda, and Ian Schreiber. 2009. *Challenges for Game Designers*. Boston, MA: Cengage Learning.

Brooks, Frederick P., Jr. 1975. *The Mythical Man-Month: Essays on Software Engineering.* Boston, MA: Addison-Wesley.

Brooks, Frederick P., Jr. 2010. *The Design of Design: Essays from a Computer Scientist.* Upper Saddle River, NJ: Addison-Wesley.

Caillois, Roger. 1962. "The Definition of Play: The Classification of Games." In *The Game Design Reader (2006)*, edited by Katie Salen and Eric Zimmerman. Cambridge, MA: MIT Press.

Church, Doug. 1999. "Formal Abstract Design Tools." Blog. *Gamasutra.* July 16, 1999. http://www.gamasutra.com/view/feature/131764/formal_abstract_design_tools.php.

Cook, Daniel. 2012. "Loops and Arcs." April 29, 2012. http://www.lostgarden.com /2012/04/loops-and-arcs.html.

CORE Team. 2017. *The Economy.* Oxford: Oxford University Press.

Costikyan, Greg. 2002. "I Have No Words & I Must Design: Toward a Critical Vocabulary for Games." In *Proceedings of Computer Games and Digital Cultures Conference*, edited by Frans Mäyrä. Tampere, FL: Tampere University Press. http://www.costik .com/nowords2002.pdf.

Costikyan, Greg. 2007. "Games, Storytelling, and Breaking the String." In *Second Person*, edited by Pat Harrigan and Noah Wardrip-Fruin. Cambridge, MA.

Costikyan, Greg. 2013. *Uncertainty in Games.* Cambridge, MA: MIT Press.

Crawford, Chris. 2003. *Chris Crawford on Game Design.* Indianapolis, IN: New Riders.

Crawford, Chris. 2005. *Chris Crawford on Interactive Storytelling.* Indianapolis, IN: New Riders.

Csikszentmihalyi, Mihaly. 1990. *Flow: The Psychology of Optimal Experience.* New York: Harper & Row.

Csikszentmihalyi, Mihaly, Sami Abuhamdeh, and Jeanne Nakamura. 2005. "Flow." In *Handbook of Competence and Motivation*, edited by A. J. Elliot and C. S. Dweck, 598–608. New York: Guilford Press.

Davies, Mark. 2009. "Examining Game Pace: How Single-Player Levels Tick." Blog. *Gamasutra.* May 12, 2009. https://www.gamasutra.com/view/feature/132415 /examining_game_pace_how_.php.

Deen, Menno. 2015. "G.A.M.E., Games Autonomy Motivation & Education: How Autonomy-supportive Game Design May Improve Motivation to Learn." Ph.D. diss., Technische Universiteit Eindhoven, Eindhoven.

DiabloWiki. 2018. "Experience Level Chart." Accessed October 23, 2018. https://www .diablowiki.net/Experience_level_chart.

Dunnigan, James F. 2000. *Wargames Handbook, Third Edition: How to Play and Design Commercial and Professional Wargames*. Lincoln, NE: Writers Club Press.

Elias, George Skaff, Richard Garfield, and K. Robert Gutschera. 2012. *Characteristics of Games*. Cambridge, MA: MIT Press.

Fenlon, Wes. 2016. "How Cats Get Drunk in Dwarf Fortress, and Why Its Creators Haven't Figured Out Time Travel (Yet)." *PC Gamer*. March 31, 2016. http://www.pcgamer.com/how-cats-get-drunk-in-dwarf-fortress-and-why-its-creators-havent-figured-out-time-travel-yet/.

Forrester, Jay Wright. 1961. *Industrial Dynamics*. Cambridge, MA: MIT Press.

Fullerton, Tracy. 2008. *Game Design Workshop: A Playcentric Approach to Creating Innovative Games, 2nd Edition*. Burlington, MA: Morgan Kaufmann.

Futter, Michael. 2017. *The GameDev Business Handbook: How to Build the Business You'll Build Games With*. London, UK: Bithell Games.

Garriott, Richard. 2017. "War Stories. Ultima Online: The Virtual Ecology." Video, 7:27. *Ars Technica*. December 21, 2017. http://video.arstechnica.com/watch/war-stories-ultima-online-the-virtual-ecology.

Greenlaw, Paul S., Lowell W. Herron, and Richard H. Rawdon. 1962. *Business Simulation in Industrial and University Education*. Englewood Cliffs, NJ: Prentice Hall. https://archive.org/details/businesssimulati00gree.

Harrigan, Pat, and Noah Wardrip-Fruin. 2007. *Second Person: Role-playing and Story in Games and Playable Media*. Cambridge, MA: MIT Press.

Harrigan, Pat, and Noah Wardrip-Fruin. 2009. *Third Person: Authoring and Exploring Vast Narratives*. Cambridge, MA: MIT Press.

Hocking, Clint. 2007. "Ludonarrative Dissonance in *Bioshock*." Blog. *Click Nothing*. Accessed October 7, 2007. http://clicknothing.typepad.com/click_nothing/2007/10/ludonarrative-d.html.

Hodent, Celia. 2017. *The Gamer's Brain: How Neuroscience Can Impact Video Game Design*. Boca Raton, FL: CRC Press.

Hunicke, Robin, Marc LeBlanc, and Robert Zubek. 2004. "MDA: A Formal Approach to Game Design and Game Research." Edited by Dan Fu, Stottler Henke, and Jeff Orkin. *Challenges in Game Artificial Intelligence: Papers from the 2004 Workshop*. Menlo Park, CA: AAAI Press.

John, Oliver P., and Sanjay Srivastava. 1999. "The Big Five Trait Taxonomy: History, Measurement, and Theoretical Perspectives." In *Handbook of Personality: Theory and Research*, edited by Lawrence A. Pervin and Oliver P. John, 102–138. New York: Guilford Press.

John, Oliver P., and Sanjay Srivastava. n.d. "The Big Five Trait Taxonomy: History, Measurement, and Theoretical Perspectives." Preprint. Accessed September 16, 2018. https://pages.uoregon.edu/sanjay/pubs/bigfive.pdf.

Juul, Jesper. 2010. "The Video Games of Video Games: Prejudices against Social Games verbatim copies of Prejudices against Video Games." Blog. *The Ludologist*. September 1. https://www.jesperjuul.net/ludologist/2010/08/31/the-video-games-of -video-games/.

Kelly, Tadhg. 2014. "Raw Game Design: You Have a Game Idea, What Comes Next?" *Game Developers Conference Next 2014*. Los Angeles, CA.

Koster, Raph. 2004. *A Theory of Fun in Game Design*. Scottsdale, AZ: Paraglyph Press.

Koster, Raph. 2005. "A Grammar of Gameplay." *Game Developers Conference 2005*. San Francisco, CA. https://www.raphkoster.com/gaming/atof/grammarofgameplay .pdf.

Koster, Raph. 2012. "A Theory of Fun: 10 Years Later." *Game Developers Conference Online 2012*. Austin, TX. https://www.raphkoster.com/gaming/gdco12/Koster_ Raph_Theory_Fun_10.pdf.

Lazzaro, Nicole. 2004. "Why We Play Games: Four Keys to More Emotion in Player Experiences." *Game Developers Conference 2004*. San Francisco, CA.

Lehdonvirta, Vili, and Edward Castronova. 2014. *Virtual Economies: Design and Analysis*. Cambridge, MA: MIT Press.

Llamasoft Ltd. 1985. "Batalyx." https://archive.org/details/Batalyx_1985_Llamasoft.

Lovell, Nicholas. 2018. *The Pyramid of Game Design: Designing, Producing and Launching Service Games*. Boca Raton, FL: CRC Press.

Madigan, Jamie. 2015. *Getting Gamers: The Psychology of Video Games and Their Impact on the People Who Play Them*. Lanham, MD: Rowman & Littlefield.

Mateas, Michael, and Andrew Stern. 2003. "Façade: An Experiment in Building a Fully-Realized Interactive Drama." *Game Developers Conference 2003*. San Francisco, CA.

Mawhorter, Peter, Michael Mateas, Noah Wardrip-Fruin, and Arnav Jhala. 2014. "Towards a Theory of Choice Poetics." *Foundations of Digital Games Conference*.

McEntee, Chris. 2012. "Rayman Origins." *Game Developer Magazine*. no. 10/2012. 26–31.

McKee, Robert. 1997. *Story: Style, Structure, Substance, and the Principles of Screenwriting*. New York: Harper Collins.

Meier, Sid. 2012. "Interesting Decisions." *Game Developers Conference 2012*. San Francisco, CA.

Norman, Donald A. 1988. *The Design of Everyday Things*. New York: Basic Books.

Pecorella, Anthony. 2016. "Quest for Progress: The Math and Design of Idle Games." *Game Developers Conference Europe 2016*. Cologne, Germany.

Reynolds, Craig. n.d. "Boids: Background and Update." Accessed September 7, 2018. https://www.red3d.com/cwr/boids/.

Ryan, Richard M., and Edward L. Deci. 2000. "Self Determination Theory and the Facilitation of Intrinsic Motivation, Social Development, and Well-Being." *American Psychologist* 55 (1): 68–78.

Ryan, Richard M., C. Scott Rigby, and Andrew Przybylski. 2006. "The Motivational Pull of Video Games: A Self-Determination Theory Approach." *Motivation and Emotion* 30 (4): 344–360.

Salen, Katie, and Eric Zimmerman. 2004. *Rules of Play*. Cambridge, MA: MIT Press.

Schell, Jesse. 2008. *The Art of Game Design: A Book of Lenses*. Boca Raton, FL: CRC Press.

Schüll, Natasha Dow. 2012. *Addiction by Design: Machine Gambling in Las Vegas*. Princeton, NJ: Princeton University Press.

Selinker, Mike, ed. 2011. *The Kobold Guide to Board Game Design*. Kirkland, WA: Open Design.

Sellers, Michael. 2017. *Advanced Game Design: A Systems Approach*. Indianapolis, IN: Addison-Wesley.

Serviss, Ben. 2013. "The Discomfort Zone: The Hidden Potential of Valve's AI Director." Blog. *Gamasutra*. February 7, 2013. https://www.gamasutra.com/blogs/BenServiss/20130207/186193/The_Discomfort_Zone_The_Hidden_Potential_of_Valves_AI_Director.php.

Sicart, Miguel. 2008. "Defining Game Mechanics." *Game Studies* 8 (2). http://gamestudies.org/0802/articles/sicart.

Skolnick, Evan. 2014. *Video Game Storytelling: What Every Developer Needs to Know About Narrative Techniques*. Berkeley, CA: Watson-Guptill.

Solarski, Chris. 2017a. *Interactive Stories and Video Game Art: A Storytelling Framework for Game Design*. Boca Raton, FL: CRC Press.

Solarski, Chris. 2017b. "The Unreliable Gamemaster: Player Motivation in Story-Driven Games." Blog. *Gamasutra*. September 9, 2017. https://www.gamasutra.com/blogs/KrzysztofSolarski/20170209/291164/The_Unreliable_Gamemaster_Player_Motivation_in_StoryDriven_Games.php.

Spolsky, Joel. 2000. "Things You Should Never Do, Part I." Blog. *Joel on Software*. April 6, 2000. https://www.joelonsoftware.com/2000/04/06/things-you-should-never-do-part-i/.

Swink, Steve. 2009. *Game Feel: A Game Designer's Guide to Virtual Sensation*. Boston: Morgan Kaufmann.

Tozour, Paul. 2013. "Postmortem: Intelligence Engine Design Systems' City Conquest." Blog. *Gamasutra*. February 6, 2013. https://www.gamasutra.com/view/feature /186088/postmortem_intelligence_engine_.php.

Upton, Brian. 2015. *The Aesthetic of Play*. Cambridge, MA: MIT Press.

Walker, Stephen F. 1975. *Learning and Reinforcement*. London: Methuen & Go Ltd.

Ward, Trent. 2003. "Ultima Online Preview." *Gamespot*. December 2, 2003. https:// www.gamespot.com/articles/ultima-online-preview/1100-2559974/.

Wardrip-Fruin, Noah, and Pat Harrigan, ed. 2004. *First Person: New Media as Story, Performance, and Game*. Cambridge, MA: MIT Press.

Wardrip-Fruin, Noah. forthcoming. *How Pac-Man Eats*. Cambridge, MA: MIT Press.

Westfall, Anne, Jon Freeman, and Paul Rieche III. 1983. *Archon* Manual. https:// archive.org/details/ArchonEAManual.

Wiener, Norbert. 1961. *Cybernetics: or Control and Communication in the Animal and the Machine, 2nd Edition*. Cambridge, MA: MIT Press.

Wittgenstein, Ludwig. 1959. *Philosophical Investigations*. Translated by G. E. M. Anscombe. New York: Macmillan.

Wolf, Maryanne. 2018. "What Does Immersing Yourself in a Book Do to Your Brain?" *Literary Hub*. August 8, 2018. https://lithub.com/what-does-immersing -yourself-in-a-book-do-to-your-brain/.

Wright, Will. 2003. *Lessons from Game Design*. YouTube video, 1:42:10. Recorded at the Computer History Museum. Mountain View, CA, November 20. https://www .youtube.com/watch?v=CdgQyq3hEPo.

Yee, Nick. 2016. "Gamer motivation profile: model and findings." *Game Developers Conference 2016*. San Francisco, CA. https://quanticfoundry.com/wp-content/uploads /2016/03/Gamer-Motivation-Profile-GDC-2016-Slides.pdf.

# Index